# from Vulnerable to Victorious

### Turning Your Chronic Illness Into Your Victory Story

## TORI JOY GEIGER

**FROM VULNERABLE TO VICTORIOUS**



ISBN: 978-1-7378189-0-8

Interior design by FormattedBooks

# Contents

# Dedication

Proverbs 31:30

"Charm is deceptive, and beauty is fleeting; but a woman who fears the LORD is to be praised."[1]

*I* dedicate this book to my dearest grandmother and paragon, Sally Marion Schroeder. During my junior year of high school, she passed away, but her legacy of godliness has been a potent driving force in my life. Displaying elegance in every endeavor, she lived out her love for Christ fervently. With a gentle spirit and prayerful living, she diligently exemplified the Proverbs 31 woman I desire to become. In her treatment of others, she exhibited integrity and a genuine concern for others. Observing her glowing tenderness and affection rooted in her devotion to Christ drives me to love

---

[1]    *Bible Hub, Bible Hub,* 2004, https://biblehub.com/niv/proverbs/31.htm.

others in such a passionate way. Throughout her life, my grandmother eloquently journaled her childhood memories and woeful circumstances, whether they humorously depicted her pet goat in her elementary years or her tumultuous battle with a thyroid storm. Thankfully today, I have the pleasure of poring over her literary works, which have motivated me to keep my own accounts of my innermost prayers and experiences with my chronic illness. Because of her prompting to develop as a wordsmith, I have rapidly grown in my love for literature and in my pursuit of excellence in writing. Due to her investment of critical wisdom in my life, I now have confidence and absolutely savor the ability I have to share my powerful personal testimony with others. Ultimately, even though my grandmother has departed this earth, her testimony to the goodness of God instills in me the character of a godly woman from whom flows class, love, and excellence.

# *Introduction*

One in 100 babies are born with a congenital heart defect (CHD).[2] Even after the most intense procedures and surgeries, this chronic illness continues to impact these individuals with continued care and supervision for the rest of their lives.

I am that one in 100. I've been that one in 100 for 23 years now, but those statistics have not defined me nor will they ever do so. I wouldn't trade my CHD and the experiences it has given me for anything. I have often been asked if I were able to be "normal" and not have a heart problem, would I want to be? There were times during my deepest frustrations and lowest points that I did wish I could just be "normal" like everyone else. During times we ran the mile in PE and I couldn't catch my breath due to my lack of oxygen, or when I

---

[2]  March of Dimes, "Congenital Heart Defects and Critical Chds," March of Dimes, June 2019, https://www.marchof-dimes.org/complications/congenital-heart-defects.aspx#:~:-text=Nearly%201%20in%20100%20babies,or%20can%20be%20treated%20easily.

found out that if I ever got serious with a significant other, I would need to tell them that their future desire for children may look different, you bet I longed to be "normal." But in the end, I think normal is overrated.

I am not going to lie and say that my heart journey has been an easy and joyous ride all the time, but I can say my life would be pretty boring without this heart of mine. Through my experiences with a chronic illness, I have developed a deeper sense of compassion, character, tenacity, and drive. Having CHD has ultimately given me a goal for my life that I never want to change, and that goal is to live a life of victory. I know what it means to work hard. I know what it is like to overcome, and I am proud of the person I have become.

One of my top 10 favorite books was written by Hal Elrod, *The Miracle Equation*.[3] Elrod's crazy life story involves overcoming an intense car crash and defeating cancer as well, and he is someone I admire immensely. My favorite section in his book talks about goals and why we set them. Often we set goals because we want to complete a task or cross that finish line to say we did it, that we achieved it. But we know so little about the person we will become to achieve that goal. Anytime

---

[3]   HAL ELROD, *MIRACLE Equation: The Two Decisions That Move Your Biggest Goals from Possible, TO Probable, to... Inevitable* (S.l.: JOHN MURRAY LEARNING, 2020).

we set an objective, achieving it involves a process of molding into a person who can obtain that goal. For someone desiring to complete a marathon, it takes a certain person, style of living, and mindset to achieve that race. During training, you become a person who can accomplish that feat. It's all in the journey, not just the finish line.

It's the same when living with a chronic illness. You have your own story filled with trials, tribulations, traumas, and hopefully lessons learned, but in the end it's not about just making it through. It's about shaping you to be the greatest version of yourself. It starts with owning your story and using it to lead a better life. And who better than those who have suffered and endured pain in such a way to lead those around them by embracing life and championing every day as a gift? How better to use your story to rise above the challenges and live your life in such a way that allows you to thrive no matter your circumstances? Maybe you are someone who has been affected by a chronic illness or some other medical ailment. We don't get to pick the set of cards this life throws at us, but we can choose not to let them define us. It takes making that conscious choice to travel beyond the mountains set before us and believe in ourselves to overcome the odds and find beauty in the life we have been given, even if that life looks very different from our peers' lives.

How we react to our circumstances plays a huge role in how we overcome the barriers in our paths. After the trauma my parents experienced with their baby girl, they could have refused to even allow me to do sports. They could have even wrapped me in metaphorical bubble wrap, but they didn't. They pushed me to have the mindset of victorious living from the start when they named me "Victoria," which quite literally means "victory." They didn't set limits for me, but rather encouraged me to knock down barriers medical professionals tried to place in front of me. Even when times were scary or the future of my health was unknown, my parents didn't let me choose to pity myself, or to wallow in self-defeat. No, I was a fighter, and I had the power to choose victory each and every day!

Now, some of you may be asking how can you *choose* victory? Isn't victory an outcome? It can be, but I think victory is more of a mindset, made up of the choices we make each day. When we embody this power of a victory mindset, we can begin to truly find the worthiness of our unique stories and find strength in our inner purpose and calling.

We have the chance to inspire and impact not only ourselves but also others as we battle through our adversity. Our stories are all composed of times when we have endured hardship. Sometimes we may have handled it well, and other times maybe not so much, but now that we have endured, we can make better choices that mold us into people that lead a victorious life.

Through stories, we get the chance to relate to one another. Today, masses of people communicate through blogging, vlogging, or podcasting through storytelling. Hosts of these media platforms are able to share their experiences with products, vacations, or life experiences, and people are interested in hearing their stories. We use the experience of people like bloggers, athletes, and successful businesses to model our behavior and choices after. I know as an athlete, I modeled my style of play after athletes I admired because I knew that was a major part in their successes. I also just love hearing other people's victory stories and the processes they went through to overcome their adversities. Stories of people like John O'Leary, author of *On Fire*, inspire me to continue to share my story because I know that it is through enduring hardship that I can lead others to live victoriously as well.

My faith also gave me the courage to write this book. God has brought me through some tremendous experiences with my chronic illness that have molded me into the woman I am today. I know wholeheartedly that within the experiences that God gives every person, he gives the ability to inspire and encourage others in their daily lives. Throughout my life, I have seen others lead extraordinary legacies, and that got me asking myself what legacy I desired to leave on this earth. What footprint would I make? I decided that I wanted to leave a legacy of victorious living through helping others like myself turn their chronic illness into their victory story.

# Chapter 1

## THE STORYLINE WE CALL LIFE

*I* believe there is a reason you are holding this book in your hand. You may be in what I call the eye of the storm, or maybe you are just coming out of it. You know what I am talking about. It's that feeling of crippling fear and worry that is overtaking you at the present moment. You feel held hostage by the belief that your circumstances can never be different, and that the cards you were dealt will never let you thrive. In fact, you might even be scared of thinking that things could get better because you know that feeling of disappointment that it could bring. You're stuck in that storm of adversity without a clear sense of direction, and in a state of overwhelm and despair. To put it bluntly, you're falling apart at the seams, hun.

Well, I get it. I have been exactly where you are. I remember it like it was yesterday.

*The crowd was roaring, and the gym lights penetrated the game atmosphere. It was a fierce game against the Blanchet Cavaliers, and we had been preparing all week for this game. As a freshman in rotation on both the JV and varsity teams, there was nothing like a big game in the rival's gym.*

*After finishing up the JV game just minutes before, I rushed over to the main gym to join the rest of the varsity in warm-ups. I had just had the game of a lifetime during that JV game: 7 three-pointers, 30 points. It was one for the record books, and I was soaring high. So was my heart. The nerves of this game and excitement of the previous one were an overwhelming feeling.*

*Cheering on my varsity teammates from the bench, standing and sitting constantly, the game intensified with every bucket and shot. Ba boom. Ba boom. Ba boom. I can still hear it in my head. My heart was racing. But I was fine, I told myself. I got this. I wanted to get in the game and get my varsity minutes in, especially coming off such a hot streak at the JV Game. Then the gym started spinning. This wasn't good.*

*I grabbed our team trainer. "Ty, something doesn't feel right. My heart is pounding uncontrollably."*

*He laid me down behind the bench on the gym floor and continued to take my pulse. You could see my heart pulsating out of my chest at this point. It was a riveting scene. My whole body was shaking from the effects of the fast-paced rhythm. It wasn't slowing down. I couldn't catch my breath. This couldn't be happening.*

*"We better call an ambulance," I heard Ty say to my dad and his training assistants. My vision was going in and out at this point, and the next thing I remember I was being rolled onto a stretcher with many curious eyes around the gym watching intensely. The doors to the ambulance shut. My dad sat on one side, and the paramedic sat on the other side.*

*"This is only going to be a pinch," the paramedic said as he hooked me up to an IV. "Can you tell me your name? How old are you? Do you remember what happened? Are you experiencing any pain in your chest right now?"*

*So many questions.*

*"I . . . I . . . I . . ." It was so hard to breathe.*

*"I am so out of breath. I can't really talk," I said as I tried to answer his questions. That must have been a trigger because the next thing I heard was,*

*"Code Blue!"*

I remember being told in high school that the moments that we experience, both trials and triumphs, shape our lives and add to the plots that make up this storyline we call life. It's in those moments of falling apart that your magnificent story of victory is coming together. While we may never want to live through trauma, we can find blessing in the journey.

Not only do I think you picked up this book because you are facing a storm. I also think you have this book in your hands because you are ready to take these experiences you are going through and turn them into your victory story. You are done being held hostage by that crippling fear that your chronic illness is controlling you with, and you are ready to overcome and live victoriously. I am here as your guide to do just that. As I share a glimpse into my own battle with a congenital heart defect, I am going to walk you through the journey of victory I have learned so that you can also experience that same power and freedom from the resiliency I already know you have within you.

It's time to grab your highlighter and a pen! I want you to mark this book up! You are on a path to victory, and I want you to underline, highlight, and note the ideas, words, and stories that impact your journey. There is also a free workbook that goes along with this book if you would like an extra resource as you read. You can find the Free Victorious Workbook at www.torijoygeiger.com/victorious. It will help guide you through moments of processing, reflection, encouragement, and more.

I am *so* excited to be on this path with you and see how you transform your chronic illness into your victory story!

Ready? Let's go!

*Chapter 2*

———∿∽᠊ᢠᢙᢘᡒᢗᢙᡒᢘᡒᢙ᠊ᢘᢀ᠊———

# TURNING "WHY ME" INTO OPPORTUNITY

When we face adversity in our lives, one of the most prominent questions we ask is "Why me?" Why was I chosen as the one to walk through this journey? Did I do something wrong? Is this punishment for something? I know sitting in the emergency room that night after my basketball game, I definitely was asking that question along with many others. That question has been a big one I've battled with through the years of living with a congenital heart defect, and I know it is something my parents truly pondered in their own lives when receiving the startling news that they were having a baby with a major chronic illness.

Every parent, upon finding out that they are pregnant, prays that their pregnancy will play out with ease and they will end up with a healthy baby. Each ultrasound is a nerve-racking yet incredible experience as the tech reveals the features of the newest addition to their family.

The year was 1997, and my parents, upon coming to their doctor's visit in our hometown, Corvallis, Oregon, were informed by their OBGYN that I might be born with heart complications. It was suggested that those complications be further examined at the Legacy Emanuel Medical Center in Portland, Oregon. During that point in my mother's pregnancy, the doctors did not mention specifics or even possibilities of any conditions I could potentially have, but anytime a doctor is concerned about a birth defect or possible complication, it's a serious matter.

Thankfully, my parents followed the doctor's orders and had more ultrasounds completed in order to truly understand any implications my birth could entail. Portland became a regular location for my parents as they attended appointment after appointment leading up to my birth.

After many ultrasounds were read and confirmed, it was ultimately determined that the right side of my heart was enlarged, along with other issues that would later be determined following my birth. Yes. God in fact did give me a "big" heart from the beginning. My mother's main OBGYN advised my parents to seek genetic counseling after all these complications were discovered, as she thought they should be prepared for any major problems that they could potentially be facing upon my arrival. With her push toward genetic counseling, it was assumed by most that I was going to be a Down syndrome baby. The OBGYN also advised my mom to get an amniocentesis, another form of testing to determine whether I had an extra chromosome, as a Downs baby would have. My parents fought the idea of having genetic counseling and performing the amniocentesis, but as young parents of an unborn child with a chronic illness, they were uncertain how to handle all of this new knowledge. It was overwhelming. No parent can ever prepare for such a circumstance.

As my parents struggled with what to do, my dad confided in my uncle's medical advice as a very trusted radiologist in Vancouver, Washington. In the simplest words, my uncle asked my dad, "Well, are you going to keep your baby if something is wrong?"

My dad answered strongly, "Well, of course."

That was the answer. Regardless of any imperfections or problems that I could have, my parents would choose to give me life and love me no matter what.

There were times that my parents asked themselves that question, "Why us?" But ultimately, even though they didn't know the reason this journey was a part of their story, they were going to look at it as an opportunity to love me no matter what. Despite the challenges, heart-ache, and unknowns, my parents made the decision to stop asking that question and start living this opportunity before them. God had entrusted them with a baby girl and a battle to fight, and even if they couldn't see it in the moment, there was greater purpose in every pain-ful moment and tribulation they knew they would face.

Once I was born, I was officially diagnosed with Ebstein's anomaly and a coarctation of the aorta. For those not familiar with these cardiac terms, Ebstein's anomaly is a rare congenital heart defect where the tri-cuspid valve of the heart does not close properly, which causes blood to leak back into the atrium of the heart. The right side of my heart is also enlarged because of this anomaly. Coarctation of the aorta means that there is a narrowing in my aortic arch, which at the time of my birth severely constricted the flow of blood to the rest of my body. At just four days old, I underwent my first open-heart surgery with an angioplasty procedure following at two months old and another open-heart surgery at seven months old.

After the last of my surgeries, my family and I re-turned to our home in Corvallis, Oregon, to face life outside of the hospital once again. Routine annual checkups became a regular part of life. I got very used to that lukewarm ultrasound jelly used at every ultrasound checkup. I still have those appointments yearly. As a young child, with *Barnie* playing in the background, I remember always watching my cardiologist's and my parents' faces as they scanned my heart on the monitor. I would try to read what they were thinking, and for some reason even as a little kid, there was always a sense of fear that something would turn up, and I would have to go through more and more surgeries. I didn't think I was ready to go through that or have my parents go through it either. Weren't we done with the tribulations? We were already overcomers, so why would God make us go through it again? That subconscious fear stayed with me through my elementary years. It wasn't something that was voiced to those around me, but it was there, and it would come out years later.

Every time I got sick, it was a very big deal because any infection could easily spread to my heart and cause many issues. Every sickness called for a pediatrician's visit. Flu shots were a must every single year for the whole family, and I hated needles. You would think they were extracting a bone from my body, I would cry so hard when the nurse came in to give me any shot. Extra precautionary drugs were taken before every dentist appointment to avoid any infection that could harm my heart. Vision therapy visits weekly down in Eugene, Oregon, (about an hour from home) became the norm for a period of my younger years as my vision was retrained. Because of the complications of my heart, my body was more focused on the trauma of my heart, and many of my facial features did not fully develop, causing the need for many months of both vision and speech therapy.

In my CHD journey, I didn't truly experience the full storm of living with a heart condition until I was in Junior High. At that time in my life, the question, "Why me?" was really on my mind. Those subconscious worries from my childhood would also eventually come out. Up until that point in my life's story, beyond my regular checkups and standard medical cautions, those tumultuous beginnings were really my parents' experiences, not my own personally, since I was so young. However, during my seventh-grade year, those tumultuous experiences quickly became my own.

One basketball practice, I suddenly felt these weird rapid-fire heartbeats as I was exercising, and I knew something didn't feel right. It just wasn't normal. Shortly after that episode, I was diagnosed with a condition known as supraventricular tachycardia. This condition entails a rapid-fire rhythmic issue that is caused when a node is formed in the heart's electrical pathway. This node was redirecting the electrical charges of my heart, causing it to beat rapidly, sometimes at 200 beats per minute, while I was just standing still. With this new condition my heart developed, I often found myself breathless, dizzy, and faint. The only way to stop the rapid-fire beating was to sit down and bear down on my heart by contracting my chest and stomach very tightly to my body. The rapid-fire episodes became a huge difficulty in athletics and a massive frustration. It was also no surprise to the doctors either that I developed such a condition because rhythm disorders were quite common with my already existing heart condition.

To combat the disorder, I was prescribed an anti-arrhythmic pill, commonly known as a beta blocker, which stabilized the beating of my heart and prevented it from firing rapidly. The only side effect was moments of fatigue and lethargy, which only occurred once in a while. After months of being on a beta blocker, I was scheduled to have a procedure known as an ablation to remove the extra node in the electrical pathway of my heart that was causing my tachycardia. That August going into my eighth-grade year, I headed up to Doernbecher Children's Hospital in Portland, Oregon, to have my first ablation. This catheter ablation involved the doctors inserting wires through the arteries in both the inside of my legs all the way to my heart. Once the wires reached my heart, the doctors were then going to remove the node off of the pathway.

Once I came out of surgery, we were informed that the surgery was successful in removing the node without any complications. However, my cardiologist warned me that it was not uncommon for another node to grow back in a different place after surgery, and therefore, I still had to be cautious about my heart and irregular rhythm episodes.

Eighth grade finally arrived with no heart complications. Playing volleyball, basketball, and softball, I learned to manage a lot on my plate. I felt like I had the world in my hands, especially when our girls' basketball team won the league championship that year. That was a pretty big deal to me. It was my first real taste of a championship experience.

It was during the championship game and start of my next softball season that I started to feel these weird flip-flop heartbeats in my chest once again. At first, I wasn't too concerned with this, since often the rhythm of one's heart is altered after procedures like the one I had just had. Then one day as I walked around my room, I almost completely blacked out. I knew something was definitely wrong.

Following that blackout event, my mom took me to our local clinic to have an EKG performed, which would then be sent to my cardiologist in Portland for further study. During the next week, the doctor had me wear a Holter monitor on my chest that recorded these weird episodes. After that, I did not hear from my cardiologist for another couple weeks. Those were some of the most suspenseful days of my life.

I still remember the feeling the day I received the news.

Sitting in class, I got a note to go to the teacher's lounge in the high school building to meet my mom. Once I arrived, I could see it written all over her face. Not good news. My tachycardia had returned, and it was worse this time.

I was devastated. That question, "Why me?" was oh so prevalent in my mind.

After my meeting with my mom, I went back to class, but on my way back I stopped at our counselor's office and just melted down. I bawled. I couldn't hold it together anymore. I couldn't believe I was back to square one.

"I trusted you, God."

I felt so let down and defeated in that moment. I could not believe this was happening to me. I had varsity athletics coming up the next year on my mind. I needed to train to be able to keep up, and this was just going to slow me down.

I was a mess that day, but that night was even more memorable for me. I received a surprise phone call from Grandma Schroeder. For those of you who may have skipped the dedication of this book, my grandma has always been a role model for me. She was such a classy woman of God, and I truly admired her.

"Hi, Victoria," she said. "I heard you had a little rough day today."

I agreed with her, and then just listened to her calming words.

"You have already overcome so much, and everything this time will be okay too. Victoria, remember Psalm 46:10, 'Be still and know that I *am* God.'"[4]

I cannot quite remember how the rest of our conversation went, but I know one thing. That verse has stuck with me through the years, and her words of wisdom were exactly what I needed to hear that day. When my grandma was failing and toward the end of her life my junior year of high school, I used to visit her and paint her nails and read Scripture to her. I read Psalm 46 to her all the time. Psalm 46:10 will forever be one of my favorite verses and memories of my godly grandmother because despite whatever I walk through, that verse reminds me that God is with me. He has a plan for every hardship I am in. Whenever I start to think "why me," I am comforted in the fact that His plans are greater than my own. I have peace in the fact that I am not alone,

---

[4]    *Bible Hub, Bible Hub,* 2004, https://biblehub.com/niv/psalms/46.htm.

and that He can use my tribulations as an opportunity to look for ways to love and bless others.

You may be experiencing these same feelings, questioning "Why me?" or "Why is this *my* story?" Let me just say, I know what you are feeling. At times, that question can just wear at you and make you feel so defeated, especially when it feels like you keep getting prognosis after prognosis. It is normal to feel and think those thoughts. While we may never understand why we are the one walking through this illness, I do know we were created by a God that loves us and has so much more for us than we can imagine. If we continue to let those "Why me?" thoughts invade our minds and never look beyond to ask the question, "What can I do with these circumstances?" we will continue to be stuck in the pit of our adversity. And that's not where we are meant to be!

The first step of claiming victory over your chronic illness is to step out of that "why me" frame of mind because it is holding you captive, friend. In my parents' example, they didn't just shake off those questions and doubts running through their heads. They reframed how they saw their adversity. Rather than this obstacle or pit, they turned it into an opportunity to love and treasure a life they had been entrusted with no matter what. You know what the good news is? You have that choice too! When you make the choice to reframe your circumstance, it doesn't mean it gets easier. I know it certainly didn't for my parents or me, but it is the first step on your road to claiming victory over your chronic illness. This step happens out of faith and resilience. And if I know anything about you reading this book, it is that you are *resilient*. You can use your chronic illness to love others in ways you are only capable of doing because you have lived through what you have. I do know that God made you for so much more, and some days the only thing we can do for our peace and comfort in this fight is just be still, and know that He is God.

Okay, now I want you to do something for me to signify this choice you are making. I want you to write the following statements. You can do this in the margin of this book, a notebook, or the free Victorious Workbook you can download at www.torijoygeiger. com/victorious. Take your pen and write the following:

"I am resilient."

"I was created to do great things. I have been entrusted with this battle. This obstacle is not my fault. Rather, it is my opportunity."

I am so proud of you! By making the choice to reframe that biting "Why me?" question into an opportunity, you are already one step closer to victory. Now, before the real battle begins, it requires the next step. It's time to lay it *all* down.

———

# Chapter 3

# I SURRENDER CONTROL

Now, you may have come to terms with reframing the "Why me?" question, but it doesn't mean the road gets easier. Well, at least at this point in your chronic illness journey. You are still living with a storm all around you, and it leaves you in fist-up fight mode most of the time. Maybe it feels more like a roller coaster than a storm, but you know what I mean. While your chronic illness may be an opportunity, that doesn't always keep your circumstances from hurting any less. And the worst part? You feel helpless. Like you have no power. You are at the will of your illness, or the next crisis situation. All you want to do is kick and scream. But unfortunately, no amount of crying, screaming, or shutting down changes your circumstances. It's truly out of your control.

*Told from my dad, Robert Schroeder's perspective:*

"As we walked you down the hall to the surgery room and handed you over to the doctors, it was one of the hardest things I ever had to do. It was out of my control and there was nothing more I could do but pray."

My mom and dad have told me about the events surrounding my complicated beginnings many times, and I don't think I truly understood the magnitude of their words until I endured my heart journey when I was already years into my life with a chronic illness. Sitting there in the emergency room after my basketball game, heart beating rapidly, I also felt that same emotion my dad expressed when my parents handed me over to the doctors. It's that realization that no matter what I do or how hard I fight it, I have *no* control. It's out of my hands.

In life, we get so used to having that control over everything we do, from the careers we choose, to the food we eat, to the people we date, but when you have a chronic illness, there are just some circumstances you can't help. I think our discomfort with our ability to not control situations comes from how we have been taught to understand control. I know in my own life, I have mistaken control as comfort. I think that because

I have an area of my life under control or the ability to control something, that there is safety and assurance in that part of my life. So when my world got rocked throughout life with the storms that came from living with a chronic illness, something I couldn't control, my first reaction was to take the reins and just keep pulling harder. But I am here to tell you, having control doesn't equate to safety or never feeling discomfort. And just because you can't control your current situation doesn't mean you can't ever change your circumstances. Because at the end of the day, we change our circumstances through our continued growth and who we become through it all. And how do we grow? You guessed it. We have to be uncomfortable. As you may already know, being pushed into the uncomfortable is a pretty common occurrence when you have a chronic illness, but you know what? Each day in that discomfort, you are growing, whether you feel it or not. The first key to enabling this growth is to stop trying to control events you have no power over, and narrow in your focus on the things you do have control over.

When my dad would tell me the story of handing me over to the doctors in the early years of my life, he would always say this phrase, "Control what you can control." It was a saying I often heard from him and athletic coaches growing up throughout my life. For instance, in basketball or volleyball games, our teams never had control over the officials and the calls they made. The only thing we had control over was our attitudes, how we treated our teammates, and how much effort we put into our performance. In your adversities with a chronic illness, you may not have control over a lot, but it's those little things you do have control over that make a big difference. Like Author James Clear says on the cover of his best-selling book, *Atomic Habits*, "Tiny Changes, Remarkable Results."[5] It's the same thing with focusing on the things we can control. Those small changes in focus create that growth during those uncomfortable times. Isn't it funny how as we surrender control we gain that comfort we seek? It's kind of backward from how our "control-craving" brains tend to think.

Now you may be asking, Tori, what do you mean? What things do I have control over? You don't know my illness. And you're right. I don't know your illness exactly, but I do know, from my experience with a chronic illness, that you definitely have control over two very important things in your life. The first one is attitude. You can control how you respond to the adverse circumstances in your life. Now, I am not saying you need

---

[5]  James Clear, *Atomic Habits: An Easy & Proven Way to Build Good Habits & Break Bad Ones* (New York City, NY: Avery Publishing Group, 2018).

to get into a froofy, false positivity, "good vibes only" state, but I am a firm believer that we can still choose to rejoice in the middle of our trials, including our chronic illness battles. It starts with the attitude of your heart. The verse that comes to my mind comes from James 1:2. It says, "Consider it pure joy, my brothers, when you face trials of many kinds."[6] I know it's not an easy battle to wake up each day with a chronic illness. The pain and discouragement is a very real thing. But because we have control over our attitude, we have the power each day to wake up rejoicing for the opportunity to be an overcomer.

The second thing you have control over is how you treat others. When we go through hard circumstances, it is so easy to snap at people or even isolate away from others. I know those are some of the reactions I have been guilty of during my experiences with a chronic illness. It's the easiest way out, and most of the time it feels the best too. You get to release your inner frustration out on your loved ones or move away physically, which is actually a representation of how you feel inside. Alone. But when we respond in those ways, we let our circumstances have all the power over us. And like I said earlier, friend, this power is in *your* hands. After all,

---

6    *Bible Hub, Bible Hub*, 2004, https://biblehub.com/niv/james/1.htm.

we inspire people through our pain, our failures, and how we handle our adversities. People aren't inspired by individuals that just have a highlight reel. I mean, do you like watching movies when nothing goes wrong for the main characters? No failures or adversity equate to straight-up boring. Those around you are watching how you get back up. When you treat others with love, respect, and kindness, even when you are going through the gauntlet, not only are you growing as a person due to the discomfort, but you are making an impact on those that are watching. You have control over how you get back up! Feeling a little more empowered? Good!

Now, I am not asking you to do anything extraordinary or astronomical, but I have another task for you to do. I want you to think about those two things in your life—your attitude and how you treat others—and I want you to repeat these phrases out loud.

"I surrender what I cannot control with my chronic illness."

"I will control what I can control in my life, which includes my attitude and how I treat others."

"I have the power to rejoice in my trials."

"I have the power to get back up each day and inspire others to do the same."

These are phrases that have helped me as reminders of what power and control I have over my chronic illness especially in those heavy, tireless times when you don't have control over a lot. Our victory over our chronic illnesses continues to prevail when we realize what we truly have power over and what we need to surrender. Once we've surrendered what we cannot control, the next step in our battles really begins—and that is learning to walk with courage.

# Chapter 9

# BANKING ON COURAGE

Often our chronic illnesses make us feel timid at times. We are already "different" than our peers, and for some of us, we commonly hear, "But you look so normal. You don't look like you have a chronic illness." Friend, raise your hand if you've heard that one before. I always think in my head when I hear that, *Well, what is "living with a chronic illness" supposed to look like?*

Growing up, I commonly heard that "you don't look like anything is wrong" from friends and family. I think that made living with a chronic illness even harder, because it made me feel like I should blend in with the rest of my peers, who were a lot different from me. Your peers' experiences and perspectives going through life are definitely not the same as yours. They don't have to monitor the things in their lives that you *have* to pay close attention to. Growing up, I had to be cautious of things like exercising, spending time in hot tubs, and drinking caffeine or sugary foods, pretty typical things other kids were doing on normal days or during birthday parties or camps. I didn't even realize it until I was in my later years of elementary school that not every kid had to take special pink chewable tablets before every dentist appointment so they didn't get sick. I thought that was just normal for everyone to do. When you are growing up with a chronic illness with many unknowns, you don't know what the next trial will be. You kind of live in this space where you are just waiting for the next prognosis, the next tribulation to hit. When you are surrounded by peers that don't have to experience similar conditions in their own lives, you can crave that "normalcy" that others have. Less risks. Less unknown.

And then when you think you have a handle on your chronic illness, you hit the teenage years. When you hit that age, when boys come into the picture and you are navigating this whole thing called hormones, life with a chronic illness takes on a whole other level. I mean, who wants to tell the boy they like about the potential risks of being with someone that has a chronic illness, or feel like they are the buzzkill that can't go hot tubbing with their friends? You are trying so hard in that time frame of life to find your identity and discover your gifts and talents, and when your dear friend, chronic illness, rears its head, it can be extremely defeating. During high school, I had some serious relationships where a future was possible, and being vulnerable about my heart condition and future risks of things like pregnancy, heart operations, and more, was one of the hardest things for me to do. I know as a teenager going through all of the changes, the craving to be normal was especially difficult for me. I remember journaling about how badly I wanted to just "be normal" like my peers. To be 16 or 17 and having to get real about these difficult things with others that have never experienced a chronic illness was scary, but it was something that I had to learn to do. It took time to develop that courage, and I owe a lot of that confidence to be an advocate for myself from my athletic journey.

I got into sports at a very young age because my older brother, Grant, was very active in athletics. Like a lot of sibling relationships, I wanted to be just like my brother. He was my hero and so good at everything he tried. From soccer to basketball to softball to volleyball, I was very active. While doctors always told us to be very cautious of any symptoms that could pertain to my heart condition, I am very thankful and fortunate that I got the opportunity to participate in athletics with my heart condition. I do know not every person walks in the same shoes when they have similar heart conditions to mine, but to say my athletic journey was "easy" or "natural" is definitely not true.

Participating in athletics with a chronic illness came with its challenges for sure. For starters, with my heart condition, my supply of oxygen was a lot less than my peers, so it was common for me to have to step out of drills from an early age. I had to definitely monitor how hard I pushed myself. There were times I had to step to the sideline, even when my teammates were working their tails off, and I had to watch them finish the drills. As someone who is super competitive like I am, that was something that was extremely hard to accept. I felt like I wasn't working as hard as my teammates. I felt weak, and to be honest, I even felt embarrassed at times. There were times I tried to hide my need to step out of drills and just keep pushing through. As you can probably figure out, that backfired pretty much every time. Because when you have a chronic illness your body knows what is enough, and it will let you know like my heart did that night after the best basketball game of my life.

Now we've come full circle to that JV Basketball Game Hot Streak that landed me in Code Blue.

*Ba boom. Ba boom. Ba boom.*

*Swish*

*Ba boom. Ba boom. Ba boom.*

My heart raced as I sprinted up and down the court shooting three after three. I was having the game of my life, as I swung down for the Blanchet Catholic Junior Varsity game that night.

Lying on the locker room floor at halftime, my heart was racing uncontrollably. When my JV coach asked how I was feeling, I shook her inquiries off as if the rapid heartbeats were nothing. I had this. This was my time to prove myself for more playing time on varsity. Boy was that a big mistake.

Back into the game I went, playing my heart out. Literally. The game finally ended in a victory for our Eagle JV team, and I was on fire.

Next, I was off to the varsity game in the big gym where I proceeded to warm up with my varsity teammates, and regain my breath, as my heart was *still* beating uncontrollably.

Then it happened.

*The game had started, and standing up from the bench, I felt as if my heart had exploded into lightning speed as I tried to brace myself.*

*"Breathe in. Breathe out. Calm," Ty, our athletic trainer, guided me. I tried and tried, but breathing this rapid fire away wasn't going to work this time.*

*Fast-forward to the emergency room...*

*Arriving at the nearby Salem Hospital, I was greeted by more doctors and rushed into the emergency room.*

*Lying on the emergency bed, I thought to myself,* This is it. This is the end. *I couldn't believe it.*

*My mom walked into the room at that moment.*

*"Read Scripture, Mom," I said weakly and fearfully.*

*If this was the end, I wanted to go peacefully listening to the Word of God.*

*My mom opened the Bible that had been sitting in the room and began to read the beginning of Psalm 23:*

*"The Lord is my Shepherd, I lack nothing. He makes me lie down in green pastures, He leads me beside quiet waters, He refreshes my soul. He guides me along the right paths for his namesake. Even though I walk through the darkest valley, I will fear no evil, for you are with me; your rod and your staff, they comfort me."[7]*

*Next the doctors entered the room, and next thing I knew, my world went black.*

*"Three, two, one, clear."*

*Shock*

*"Clear."*

*Shock*

*"Clear."*

*Shock*

---

[7]    *Bible Hub, Bible Hub,* 2004, https://biblehub.com/niv/psalms/23.htm.

*Ba boom. Ba boom. Ba boom. Ba boom.*
*Unsuccessful.*

Yes, that happened. And yes, I was defibrillated three times in order to get my heart back into its normal rhythm. Finally, after the three failed attempts, the doctors fed a strong antiarrhythmic drug into my IV in order to calm my heart down as a last resort to avoid my heart going into cardiac arrest. Slowly, but surely, it worked as my heart's rhythm wound down over the following hours.

That was probably the scariest moment of my life where I came so close to what I thought was the end of my life. It took months of going to therapy to deal with the PTSD I was diagnosed with from the entire experience. And while I know there are a lot of factors that played into this event in my life, I do know there was one thing I was in control of, and that was being an advocate for myself. I shouldn't have shrugged off my coach's inquiries. I should have listened to my body, but my pride took over. My desire to be "normal" and to be perceived as a "winner" by my coaches and teammates drove me to keep going and ignore the risks right in front of me.

I know that growing up, it was easy to feel like I was just not being mentally tough and that is why I couldn't finish drills and needed to step out of activities, but when you live with a chronic illness like a heart condition, your "pushing it" looks different than your peers'. And you know what? That's *okay*! Let me tell you a little secret, you can *still* be a successful athlete! It just takes a little more creativity in training and in mentality. It also takes courage to stop when you need to.

I had to learn that by continuing to push myself past what my heart was able to do at that training period in my athletic career, I was doing more harm to myself than good. Friend, I am going to say this, and I want you to truly remember this: You *have* to be an advocate for yourself. Whether that is with teachers, coaches, friends, or teammates, being a voice for your chronic illness is so important. Do not hide it. I think that was a huge part of my success in athletics. Over time, I became more bold and able to stand up and say something when I felt odd or when I knew I shouldn't push it further. Let's get this straight. You are not weak when you have to stop or opt out. You *are* mentally tough. You know why you are mentally tough? You know your body so well, you are able to set boundaries to protect your health, something most people don't know how to do! And I will be frank, for the teammates, friends, or coaches that don't understand your chronic illness or give you a hard time about not being able to keep up, that's their own problem and immaturity. You do not need to feel guilty, not good enough, or inferior to your peers because you are created differently. The best coaches and teammates are the ones that are willing to invest in you and will work with you to develop ways you can train that better suit your illness's current limits. I have been blessed over my athletic career to have been on those teams and be coached by amazing individuals that saw past my chronic illness to a heart that wanted to be the best it could be with their help. What I found along my athletic journey is that as I trained in a way that was healthy and suited to my heart's pace, I gradually exceeded those limitations I previously had. It might mean spending some extra time in the gym or on the field outside of your typical practices, but it starts with embracing courage to be an advocate for yourself no matter how you fear others will respond. Do not let pride or the fear of rejection stop you from exercising this courage. Just remember, battling a chronic illness makes you one tough cookie, and by living with this chronic illness, you are an overcomer. When you need a little confidence boost in order to advocate for yourself, never forget that.

Now it's your turn to be an advocate. I want you to write down three ways that, starting today, you can practice this courage and be an advocate for yourself. These ways can be as simple as "I am going to be more open with my coach about my condition and how I need their support in my athletic journey," or "I will be vulnerable with my friends about my condition and the limitations I have."

You are courageous, my friend. The courage is in there, and at times, I know it may not feel like you have courage, but every time you stand up for yourself, you are putting a deposit in your confidence bank. And over time, it will get easier to be an advocate and be vulnerable with those around you.

As you develop this courage, you will need to give that courage direction, and that starts with defining your purpose.

*Chapter 5*

————◦◦◦◦◦◦————

# SHOOT WITH PURPOSE

*P*utting those small deposits of courageous moments in your confidence bank will add up over time, and now it's time to put that courage into action. It's time to start thinking about your purpose.

Growing up, my dad was my coach in many sports, but our favorite sport to do together was basketball. From the time I was in fourth grade all the way through sixth grade, I competed in the annual Elk's and Knights of Columbus Free Throw Shooting Competition at a local high school. (I even won a state championship at Knights of Columbus shooting 23/25 free throws as a fifth grader.) I can still hear in the back of my head today, my dad saying, "Victoria, shoot with purpose:

fingertip control, back spin, follow through." It was easy as a youngster to get frustrated when I couldn't make shots, and it was "easier" to just chuck up a shot and hope it went in. Shooting with purpose required more focus and intention to every detail. In the same way, defining our purpose adds intentionality to our lives. There is no more "hoping and wishing" that everything we throw up on the wall of life will stick. When we truly take the time to define purpose, we allow ourselves to direct the energy of every courageous act into that higher purpose.

I think the word "purpose" can scare people. Often people use the word purpose interchangeably with "calling." That word can be scary too. I know as a teenager if someone was to ask me "What is your purpose?" I would have responded with the cliché Christian response, "Spread the good news of Jesus Christ." And while that is the foundation and my ultimate purpose here on this earth, I think that within that overarching purpose, I have been given multiple callings in my life, from being a business owner to making an impact on those that are living with chronic illnesses. I think even at a young age, it is important to probe into the purposes God has given our lives. These purposes evolve as we get older, develop new skills, or discover talents we didn't know we had. Trust me, you are not limited in what your purpose can be! The important thing is to start thinking and defining what you believe your purpose is. Now, I am not saying your purpose has to be something enormous like world peace or ending world hunger. I think people tend to think that their purposes have to be insanely extraordinary things, but I am here to tell you that your purpose could be as simple as being the best listening ear to those that need a friend or comforting hug.

Instead of thinking of purpose in its typical "extraordinary" context, think of purpose as "who I would like to become." As I mentioned in the introduction of this book, one of my favorite authors is Hal Elrod, and in his book, the *Miracle Equation*, he talks about why he started training for an Ironman, reading, and forming certain habits.[8] He explained that he did those things because he wanted to be the type of person that could do those things. He wanted to have the character qualities of someone who competes in an Ironman. Things like mental toughness and grit. I found his book so encouraging, I even took up long-distance running (something that has *never* been my thing, and is really hard for me) because I decided I wanted to be the type of person who ran. I wanted to develop a thicker skin

---

[8]   HAL ELROD, *MIRACLE Equation: The Two Decisions That Move Your Biggest Goals from Possible, TO Probable, to... Inevitable* (S.l.: JOHN MURRAY LEARNING, 2020).

in business and more grit to make it through some challenging times I was facing as a business owner. And you know what? By defining who I wanted to become (my purpose behind my actions), I kept going and getting better! I not only completed a half-marathon with my sister-in-law, but I also became a better businesswoman in the process.

Now it's your turn. Take out your pen, workbook, and/or notebook and start jotting down some character qualities you would like to have. Maybe those things are qualities like, "I want to be a better listener," "I need thicker skin," "I want to be more thoughtful of others." Start with those qualities. Next, if you were to become a better listener, have thicker skin, or were more thoughtful, what would that look like in your life? Would you be happier or more satisfied in your relationships? Would it make work or your business easier and equate to less worrying? Describe to me in this section how you would feel if we were living each day with those character traits as a part of who you are.

Now, the last thing I want you to do is write down one to three ways you can take action to develop these traits. Think outside the box on this. Maybe running or meditation can help with developing a thicker skin or sending a note to a significant other or friend is a step to becoming more thoughtful. It's all up to you, and in taking action on these things, you are helping launch yourself into the purpose you are chasing.

Hooray! You've started to define your purpose, that person you want to become! That is *huge*! Once you have established that purpose and those important steps, you are ready to surround yourself with a team to help you keep moving forward toward that purpose!

Meet your victory tribe.

# Chapter 6

———∿∽⊙⟨⊙⟩⊙∽∿———

# YOUR VICTORY TRIBE

hey say that you become most like the five different people you surround yourself with. Or like
my dad would tell my brother and I growing up,
"If you hang out with poop, you'll start to smell like
it." That always created some giggles from my brother
and me at an early age, but it couldn't be more true. It
is something that has stuck with me throughout life. I
have always been pretty selective in who I hung around
growing up, because I knew it made an impact. When
you have a chronic illness, who you surround yourself
with makes all the difference in the world.

If you choose to spend your time with negative
nannies or people who do not respect the boundaries
you have set with your chronic illness, you will see

the effects of it. Guaranteed. Going back to Chapter 4, if you are around friends or teammates that do not truly respect your chronic illness in its entirety, do not waste your time trying to build relationships with those people. Instead, look to surround yourself with people that are your encouragers, biggest cheerleaders in the midst of the fight, and those that will challenge you to be better. These people will not only support you when it gets tough, but they will also challenge you when needed. This starts with your family, the people who have battled your chronic illness with you from day one.

Now, I know everyone's family dynamics are different, but I know for me growing up, my older brother, Grant, was that person that could challenge me to see circumstances and decisions differently. We didn't always get along in our younger years, but when times got really tough, he was always my biggest fan helping me fight. He still to this day pushes me to be the best version of myself even when I am in the midst of a hard-fought battle.

*Told from Grant Schroeder, Tori's older brother's perspective:*

Buzz…

Buzz…

We were in the car driving home from the Blanchet game when the phone rang.

"Victoria has collapsed and is being taken by ambulance to the Salem Hospital."

It was an instant flood of emotions all at once. Surprise. Fear. Confusion. It was one of those instant gut-punch moments that throws you into the reality of life. The longer we drove, the more fear set in as we made our way to the hospital.

Once we arrived, it felt like forever to find parking as we were rushing to her room in the ER. Trying to remain calm with emotions racing was a task threatening to overtake me by the minute. It was an emotion I really do not ever want to experience again.

Finally finding the right room, I (Grant) waited just outside as all the medical professionals swarmed in and out of the room while my parents stood along her side. I could see Victoria hooked up to bundles of wires, her vitals being checked constantly. Doctors were crowding all around her bedside. I felt completely helpless. It was out of my hands. There was nothing I could do . . . but pray.

Then they brought out the defibrillator pads.

*"Three, two, one, clear."*

*Shock.*

I guess the magnitude of the circumstances didn't really hit me until they brought out the defibrillator, and I saw Victoria's body jolt off the bed.

I couldn't take it. I lost it. I was certain I was losing my baby sister.

Staying in the waiting room until things subsided felt like forever, but Victoria was stable enough to comfort the raging fears that had been present all night. Since I had school the next morning, my parents had me leave to spend the night with friends. I didn't want to leave the hospital without knowing that Victoria was going to be okay.

There were no words to describe my feelings as I left the hospital. I was just in shock. I had almost lost my sister, and I couldn't appreciate her precious life more than I did at that moment. I went to school late the next day, still so numb. I lost count of the number of people coming up asking how I was doing. They all truly cared so much about Victoria and our family, and for that, I am truly grateful.

Growing up, I never thought of Victoria as different or saw her as the victim of her circumstances. We were raised to be achievers. The best we could be. My mom and dad never placed limits or labels on either of us no matter the challenges we faced. I do remember going to regular checkups as a family and experiencing the built-up anticipation when waiting on results or important appointments. I felt the concerns with the ablations and waiting to see if Victoria's heart would stop her rapid-fire heartbeats. We were all there experiencing the frustration when Victoria's first ablation wasn't successful. We took every "win" and "loss" as a family and were there to celebrate every victory. We just wanted Victoria to continue to live life with no boundaries or fears, and that's just what she continues to do.

When people ask me about Victoria's heart, it is always hard to explain to people. She is a fighter; her name means Victory. I love the fact that my mom gave both of us names with meanings. Grant: great. Victoria: victory. The fact that doctors told her she probably would never play sports was just more fuel on her fire of victory.

She played three sports in high school, and you never would have known she had anything holding her back. That's the way she lives life to this day.

The fear of losing her was very real, but we didn't let it slow down our lives or ambitions. Just like other CHD babies, Victoria is a miracle baby. Just looking at her, you would not even know the battles she has gone through. She has achieved more than most have even without heart problems. I am so proud to see her continue that achievement today through fitness, business, real estate, etc. She always finds a way to overcome the obstacles in her path.

As a family affected by CHD, we are so much closer as a family. It's a bond that's truly hard to explain. My mom and dad were always there for both me and

Victoria. I guess you could summarize it as "they always showed up for us." We always knew we were loved and valued. Oh, yes, they were hard on us at times. They disciplined and taught us each and every day. The thing that stands out the most for me is also something I greatly desire to be able to do for my kids one day. I can honestly count on my fingers less than 10 times that I did not have at least one parent at my sports games throughout my career from little league all the way through college.

Life and time with one another are never taken for granted in our family. You simply do not take anything for granted when you truly know just how precious life is around you. I think we were more involved in each other's lives than other families around us, and through that, we grew stronger. My biggest advice for siblings and families watching your loved one battle adversity is just showing up. Be there. Let them know how valued they are by giving not just your words, but your time. It makes all the difference.

Tori here.

I shared with you my brother's experience because I think it is important to get an inside scoop on what a victory tribe looks like, and I think Grant summarized it the best. It is taking every "win" and "loss" as a team and celebrating every victory. When you have a chronic illness, the easiest inclination is to isolate yourself from others. I know this is especially true for me as the introvert that I am. It seems easier to try to fight your chronic battles by yourself. I have felt that. The last thing you want to do is burden others with the problems you are facing, but the truth is we were not made to walk through storms by ourselves. Your strength is multiplied by having other people surrounding you and supporting you as you navigate the rough waters. Maybe you already have those people in your life that you lean on as you battle your chronic illness. That is great! Keep fighting together. But maybe you are in a different boat. Maybe you are still looking for those people to surround yourself with. Those people that are going to share your wins and losses. That's okay! You can form these friendships with teammates, friends, coaches, or teachers. I know it can seem like these types of "victory" people are hard to find, especially when you are going through your teenage years, but I promise you this: Those partners are out there and ready to support and encourage you. It may take some effort to form those relationships in your victory tribe, but over time those people will be growing right alongside you.

My victory tribe has changed over the years as I have grown up and life chapters have turned, and I am so blessed to experience this chronic illness journey with all the different individuals that have been such important instruments in my life. For me, my victory tribe started with my family, but over the years that team also evolved into deep friendships, teammates, coaches, and eventually a spouse. It has been that friend that reminded me who I was when I went through a bad breakup or a disappointing doctor's visit. It was that teammate that trained with me. It was the coaches that continued to believe in my potential as an athlete and invested the hours in me to make sure I reached it. Those were the types of people that truly helped me achieve victory every day. I couldn't be more grateful for my tribe.

If you are in a place in life where you are still looking to find these individuals, I highly encourage you to get involved in community groups at places like a local church or organization. You can even connect with other individuals going through similar battles through social media. I think that is one of the positives that comes out of the technology-driven world we live in! You could start with looking up the hashtag on Instagram #chronicillness to find others fighting similar battles. I know for CHD, there are many Facebook groups and nonprofit organizations that have groups to join and connect with others. You can even join my closed Facebook Group called TJG Victory Tribe by heading to www.torijoygeiger.com/victorious to find other women affected by chronic illness. Those are great places to start and find people of similar values and even similar battles if you choose to get involved with an organization that relates to your chronic illness.

My CHD experience made my family so much tougher and pulled us together. Growing up, I had my tribe of people who believed in me when obstacles came down the road. I was never facing them alone. Our family has what Angela Duckworth would call true grit.[9] My experience affected all of us. My parents had to give up control as they handed me over to surgeons and specialists. They had to relearn how to raise a more "medically afflicted" child. My brother had to grow up alongside all the medical attention being on me. He walked through the suffering with me, even through the trauma of seeing me get defibrillated right in front of him. Nothing like a real electric shock to make you realize the gift of life and express gratitude for everyday life with your loved ones. But out of all my experiences, I gained my biggest fans and best friends. We were in it to gain each victory together.

Now it's your turn. Can you think of those people who are fighting alongside you? Maybe that's a family member or close friend? I want you to write down their names in your workbook/notebook and then shoot

---

[9]    Angela Duckworth, *Grit: The Power of Passion and Perseverance* (New York City, NY: Scribner, 2018).

them this little text: "Thank you for being a part of my victory tribe."

By doing this, you are acknowledging the role they play in your journey. It's so important to let them know how much you value their support and encouragement.

If you are in that stage of life where you are still looking for people to fill that victory tribe, I want you to write down one to three ideas of places you could get involved in where you could find individuals with similar values. This could be as simple as joining your local Bible study, finding an online community group of those battling chronic illness, or volunteering at an animal shelter serving alongside incredible like-minded animal-loving people. It is totally up to you and the victory tribe you desire to form! If you have people in your life asking how they can best support you, you can share the excerpt in this book that is told from my brother's perspective, if it is something that resonates with you.

As you build your victory tribe, you will multiply your strength in the fight against your chronic illness. This doesn't always mean that your circumstances get easier, but it does get easier to stand back up from every stumble when you have a victory tribe lifting you up.

# Chapter 7

---

# LET IT ALL OUT, HONEY

While living with a chronic illness, you experience many highs and lows. Sometimes those highs are so high you forget about what you have battled through so far. I definitely remember at times feeling like I was "normal" when the waters were calm. And just when you think things are looking up or you have everything figured out, you get a new prognosis or an episode occurs that feels like it sets you back miles behind where you had just been. That was how I felt the morning after I had been rushed to the ER and defibrillated on that scary night following my dramatic exit from my basketball game. It didn't take long for anger to set in.

Soon after being stabilized by an antiarrhythmic drug, it was about two in the morning when I was transported by ambulance to OHSU in Portland, Oregon, for further attention and consultation with my cardiac rhythm specialist and pediatric cardiologist.

After spending that night in Portland, I was sent home the next day after being cleared as stable and able to return to normal activity. At this point in time, another ablation had been scheduled to take place later in the month to hopefully correct these traumatic rhythm problems. After just that eventful night, the thought of another ablation and returning to the hospital petrified me.

I did not want to go back. I did not want to sit in another hospital. I would be out of normal activities for another week after my surgery, and I was already missing so much. Besides, my tachycardia was just going to come back like it did before. This was something I definitely believed. I thought what I was experiencing was God's punishment. How could He do this to me?

Everyone was telling me how fortunate I had been, and how God had been watching over me, since I didn't die from cardiac arrest that night, but I could not see it. How was I lucky? It felt like everything was being taken away from me. I felt weak and embarrassed to show others that "weakness." It was easy to put on a nice face and pretend like everything was grand. Saying things like, "God has a plan," was easy to say to people but a completely different battle to actually believe for myself.

I didn't even want to set foot on a basketball court let alone touch a basketball. It was all God's fault. He was demolishing my athletic dreams and my ability to have a "normal" life right before me. Hospitals now terrified me. I was furious and so confused.

What if I never got to play basketball again—or any sports, for that matter? All my hard work over the years would have been for nothing. I didn't know what I would do without sports. Sports, in that phase of my life, were my identity, and that identity would never be the same for me if I couldn't go on playing. Panic really began to sink in.

My next surgery fast approached later in the month, but I was still bitter toward God. I remember going home that night after my second ablation when the anger and confusion came out, all at once. I just snapped.

My parents were having a conversation, talking about the day and the next steps we were going to have to take.

"How are you feeling, Tori?" they inquired.

"What do you think?" I sarcastically proclaimed from the back seat.

"Hey now," My dad said calmly. "That's no way to respond."

"God did this to me. He is ruining everything. Why can't I just be normal? I hate Him for this." My heart cried out as I said this.

My parents sat there in silence.

I couldn't believe the words that had just come out of my mouth. I said it. All of my pent-up bitterness, insecurity, and fear was released. Fear I believe was still there from my childhood years. It was all coming out. I knew that I shouldn't be mad at God. I just was. I blamed him, and I blamed myself. I could not understand why all this was happening to me. I had lived as a "good Christian." I had not done anything wrong. I had been such an overcomer in the past. Where was God now? If He had saved me at such a young age and given me victory then, what was He doing now?

I thought, *This was not supposed to be a part of my story. My story was what I overcame as a baby and how I am doing so well years later. What am I supposed to tell people now?* It looked to me like God had failed me. My body had failed me.

I cannot say that my anger toward God was just gone after that incident and all was healed. My physical heart may have been fixed, but my spiritual heart was still broken and in major need of repair for many months. I went through a time where I didn't really want to talk to God about what I was facing. Many of you have probably felt the same way. You feel alone, punished, and you cannot understand the reason behind facing these storms and trials again, especially after you thought the rocky road had ended.

Slowly, but thankfully, I was able to return to basketball, and upon my return, I even got a round of applause the first JV game I subbed into. That was kind of a cool experience. Later, our varsity team went on to make it to the state playoffs and ended up finishing eighth in the state.

To be honest, it was around that time my heart began to soften. I spent hours talking to my mom and mentors about what was going on, and I even visited a counselor to get through the trauma I had experienced at the awful night of the basketball game. The counseling helped pull me through the PTSD I was experiencing, but it was during those sessions with my counselor, mentors, and my mom that I made many realizations about the events that occurred that year.

I had been putting sports before everything. It was my life. My claim to normalcy. My everything. But my life could not thrive that way, and God knew it because I wasn't made to just be an athlete. He had created me for more. Those athletic gifts were His gifts to me, not something I could do myself.

From the start of high school, life seemed perfect, and I had control of my life. That was it. I was in control. I was not allowing the one who knew best to give me direction. I was doing life my way. Flashing back to Chapter 3, I had forgotten what I could and couldn't control. The funny thing is I had even started to really treat myself like I was normal, the same as everyone else. But I am not. God created me differently.

My purpose was to show God's victory and power through my life, and love others through it even if that wasn't through athletics. It was almost like I had forgotten that I needed God and the role he played in how far I had come, the true power behind my victory.

Wow.

The one who has been there from the beginning. The one who saved my little heart's life in those early surgeries, has never let me down, or given me a reason to doubt Him. In fact, I acted like I didn't need Him, and I got mad at Him when He reminded me that I needed Him to live life victoriously.

When my identity became wrapped up in all that I could do, God was left out of the picture. Out of my identity. The victory identity He had given me from the beginning. While I was mad at God after my surgery, I was fearful of how others would perceive me once I lost this identity that was wrapped up in my athletic abilities. I had forgotten Galatians 3:26 that "In Christ Jesus you are all children of God through faith."[10] I believed that I would be a nobody with nothing to offer. But that wasn't true. That was a lie from the enemy. The love and grace of Jesus Christ is my identity, not the gifts He gave me to glorify Him. He is the one that is ultimately giving me my victory. That was something I had to get straight as I processed my charged emotions.

Let me also start off by saying, anger and confusion with your chronic illness are perfectly normal. They are valid emotions that you feel as you are processing the events before you. Never forget that. I used to feel so ashamed of my car outburst with my parents and really revealing those "ugly" feelings I was experiencing during those circumstances. It felt like I had to put on a good face, and maybe you are going through that too. It's okay to not hold it together. It's okay to express those emotions. Ugly or not. That is why you have your victory tribe. They are there when you are triumphing, and they are there to help you process those emotions. When we are able to share the anger and confusion we are feeling, we are not only better at processing our chronic illnesses, we are also growing in those moments. We are able to explore our circumstances clearer

---

10    *Bible Hub, Bible Hub*, 2004, https://biblehub.com/niv/galatians/3.htm.

with no veil over our eyes, and getting back on our feet is easier.

When we express those real and raw emotions, it is a step to getting back up from those circumstances that knock us out, right flat on our butts. And after we have laid it all out on the table, it is then time to start getting back on our feet. If there is anything I have learned about living with a chronic illness, it's that it doesn't matter how many times we get knocked down. Because we *will* get knocked down. We *will* forget what we have control over. It's how we handle those blows and those emotions of anger and confusion. That is the key to us continuing to fight victoriously against our chronic illness. For me, getting back up from the anger I felt after my traumatic episode entailed truly reflecting on the way I was living my life. From reflecting on those things, and making realizations about how I had been trying to control every piece of my life, I was able to make changes in my priorities and how I saw my life. Returning to the foundation of my identity as a daughter of Christ surrounded by the grace and love of God was something I needed to do in order to grow and keep claiming victory over my illness.

I don't know the exact things you are learning from the setbacks or storms you are facing with your chronic illness, but I do know this: I know you are learning and growing despite your battles. You may not even realize it, but you are getting tougher by the minute. You will get back up, and that's what counts. I am claiming that for you! Now you need to claim it too!

To claim this, I want you to write down these three affirmations in your workbook or notebook.

"I am more than my setbacks."

"I know I will stumble and fall at times, but I will keep getting back up."

"The emotions I feel in this journey are real and valid. They do not define me as a person, but rather they empower me to heal in the process and claim victory over my illness."

Friend. I am so excited for you! Recognizing and validating the emotions you feel even when they feel ugly at times is so important. Like I said earlier, it doesn't matter how many times you get knocked down in this journey; it is all about how you continue to get back up. And how you get back up is a choice that only you have the power to make.

So how do we continue to make that choice while we are in the pit? It's actually pretty simple and sweet, and it starts with having a heart of gratitude.

# Chapter 8

—◦◦◦—

# THE CATALYST
# OF GRATITUDE

*B*eing able to get out of the pit of fear, anger, and confusion with your chronic illness starts with practicing simple gratitude. You might be thinking, *But I am not grateful for my chronic illness.* That is totally okay. I am in no way saying that you need to be all in love with your chronic illness. No, you don't have to feel that way at all toward your chronic illness, but you can be grateful for other things in your life. And I guarantee, by getting into a practice of expressing simple bits of gratitude, you will be able to get up a lot quicker each time you get knocked down.

The simple power of gratitude amidst hardship has actually been scientifically proven to help us better face and process our adversity. It allows us to get our minds off of our circumstances, and by being able to do that, we are strengthening our minds to better face adversity. It also gives us mental clarity, and I don't know about you, but when I am going through the storm, my mental state can get quite foggy. It's easy in those seasons to think that you have nothing in your life to be grateful for.

I know when I'm sitting in that hospital room as nurses poke and prod me with each test, every needle, every blood pressure test, it is overwhelming. Even though I have been through many surgeries and have been around needles my entire life, *I still to this day dread them.* When I am in those uncomfortable moments, those moments of overwhelm, I close my eyes and remember my gratitudes and pray. This intentional practice of gratitude has been huge in my life and has truly been such a *big* part of my journey with a chronic illness. Not only has the practice of gratitude helped me in times of distress, but it has also helped me release a lot of the pain I have felt in my journey. I *do* have good things in my life, and in the storm, it may be harder to remember those things, but they *are* there!

As I explained earlier, I had to process through the fear, anger, and confusion I felt after my scary episode in the ER, and in the reflections I had on my life thus far, I had to return to a heart of gratitude, whether I realized it or not. In my return to gratitude, I had to express these gratitudes like: I am grateful for the opportunity to participate in athletics. I am grateful for loving friends, family, and teammates that care about me. I am grateful for a roof over my head, food on my plate, and a warm bed to sleep in. I am grateful for the doctors I have had in my life that have played such a role in keeping me healthy and active. These things may seem super simple, but they are things I definitely needed to express in that time of my life in order to overcome the storm. Sometimes we are only able to utter the simplest gratitudes because we are in such a place of pain from a hard-fought battle. I've been there. It's not innately the first thing we think of, so it's by no means easy. But when we take the time to express our gratitude in everyday life and *even* in the storm, it does get easier to do so over time as new storms come about. As with everything else in life, it takes practice to make it stick.

Expressing gratitude can become a habit you build in your life, and it can become second nature. You can start expressing gratitude by just writing down things you are grateful for in a journal. That is something I personally do, and it is one of the most rejuvenating and refreshing activities for me during the day. In my gratitude journal, I express my gratitude for big and small things from my comfy bed to the relationships and dreams in my life. If you need a little prompting on some gratitude items, I have a list of 100 gratitude prompts to get you started in the Victorious Workbook. You can use these gratitude prompts as you begin your own gratitude practice.

If you want to take it a step further with your gratitude practice, you can actually speak your gratitude. This takes a bit more boldness, but the impact is immense. Whether that is shooting a text, email, or saying it out loud to someone, you can verbalize your gratitude for others around you. It is as simple as saying, "I appreciate you and am grateful to have you in my life."

If you are feeling even bolder, try telling a stranger something you are grateful for about them. Maybe it's the mailman delivering your mail. "I am grateful for the job you do." Or maybe it's your local barista or checkout clerk at your grocery store. Saying a simple, "Thank you for all you do. I am grateful for you," is so impactful on both you and the person you have just expressed your gratitude to, and let me tell you, gratitude creates a ripple effect! When you verbally express your gratitude, you will have just set off a chain reaction!

Maybe you aren't quite at the place where you feel comfortable shooting that text or complimenting a total stranger. No problem! There are lots of other ways you can express gratitude, and one other way I have found helpful is in serving.

When I was in the hospital undergoing my heart procedures, my parents stayed at the local Ronald McDonald House in Portland near the hospital. For those of you who are not familiar with Ronald McDonald Houses, these houses are located near hospitals, and they provide a place to stay for families of children from birth to 21 years of age. They provide comfort and relief to parents like mine who need to be close to their hospitalized child. Basically, they are a home away from home for families traveling from afar as their child undergoes procedures or has to stay in the hospital.

Growing up, I always remember seeing home videos and pictures of my family and extended family at that house, and to be honest, I was so jealous they all got to stay at this fun house with its amazing play structures and all. As I got older, I got more interested in trying to give back to places that have been a part of my journey as a CHD patient, and Ronald was one of the first places I got involved with. One of the ways I enjoy most when it comes to expressing gratitude is by serving meals at that same Ronald that my parents stayed at. It has been such a blessing to go and prepare meals for the current families staying there and just sit and talk with them. I have brought classmates, family members, and friends to come serve alongside me, and serving in that way in a place that was a home away from home for my family is one of the most rewarding experiences. It is one of the greatest ways I express my gratitude for the things I have overcome in my life.

Maybe you have an organization that has been impactful for you, or maybe there are various causes you are passionate about helping. Well, one of the easiest ways to practice your gratitude in life outwardly is by getting involved. Not only are you expressing your gratitude, but you are also making an impact on others around you.

Forming habits of gratitude is transformational during chronic illness, and it is one of the best tools we have as we continue to face the adversities that come our way. It is easy to get stuck in that pit of anger and confusion. We all do at times, but the important question is "How do we get back up?" And now, you know. You can use your practice of gratitude however it best fits you to keep on getting back up every time! And the best part about this practice of gratitude? This gratitude you exude in your life will then set your foundation to not only get back up but to also launch you into your future.

*Chapter 9*

—⁓꙰꙰꙰⁓—

# BE THE DREAMER

*W*hen you have established your foundation in gratitude, you are able to better look into the future with confidence and vision. And what I mean by this is that you are able to dream *bigger*. You are able to get your eyes off your chronic illness for long enough to think about your desired future. While this may seem froofy to some, I know for a fact that dreaming big has been a *huge* part in me overcoming limitations set forth by my chronic illness. I think too often we stop dreaming at a very young age, especially if we have a chronic illness, because our futures are so unknown and the present realities we go through don't always make us want to think about the future. I totally get that. But let me tell you, while you may not know what the future may bring, we do know who holds our future, and He does have plans for you to prosper. Even though we don't know what that looks like, I believe that we are each given dreams in our hearts, and God honors our desires to fulfill those dreams because it is a testament to His goodness and power when we go after those dreams.

My parents always called me a dreamer growing up, and when I set my mind to something, I went after it. Even with my CHD, I didn't see limits or boundaries to my future. To me, it just seemed like it was right in front of me. As a kid, I was constantly coming up with businesses or ways to earn extra money. When I was in fifth grade, my desire to be a businesswoman really began. It was around that time I also learned the term "dividend" from flyers and signs I saw at my local bank. To my little mind's understanding, you gave your money to a big company like Nike and they paid you for owning it. Well, sounds like I sort of got it right? Not quite. I thought I would give Nike $10, and they would pay me back $100 for owning their stock. Wow, wouldn't that be nice of them? My favorite business I have ever come up with was all around this idea of dividends. Those that know me know I *love* dogs, especially golden retrievers. Today, I am in love with our adorable goldendoodle, Teddy! This said, I was constantly asking my parents to get a golden retriever puppy, and with us already owning a border collie, my parents always quickly said, "No." So I had a plan. I can still feel the same adrenaline I felt then with the business ideas I think of today. My best friend, Ashley, and I were going to own a golden retriever puppy business! Best idea ever! Then we could play with puppies all the time! I dreamed and dreamed of having this "puppy business." We thought it was the coolest thing ever. Basically, we came up with the idea of being a breeder without knowing it. If we could make money, my parents couldn't possibly say no, right? But how were we going to fund it? Well, of course, we could use dividends! Being a huge fan of Build-A-Bear at that age, I came up with the genius idea to invest in Build-A-Bear stock. We could then use the dividends they paid us to start our business. We were so smart. I knew it. We scoured the internet and went right to the Build-A-Bear website to buy their stock. We even searched for it on their website. Sadly, our little business plan was interrupted by my mom coming in the back bedroom to find us on the internet without permission. That soon ended our research, and our little business idea was set aside. Oh well. It was a solid attempt.

That same tenacity and determination to go after dreams from a young age stuck with me as I journeyed through my high school years, even through the tribulations I faced my freshman year of high school that basketball season. The fall before that freshman basketball season, I had had the privilege of getting some playing time on the varsity volleyball team as well. At my high school, Santiam Christian, volleyball was a top athletic program and a well-known "dynasty," as it was called by many around the state. My head coach, Kim Mclain, had produced many excellent collegiate players that went on to have successful careers. Her coaching influence has impacted many in the realm of volleyball.

In fact, 2011, my freshman year of high school, was the three-peat state championship year for the program, and our team was itching to make school history. The previous year as an eighth grader, I had been in attendance for the two-peat state championship, and I very well knew the pressures I was up against the next year. I had always looked up to the SC girls' volleyball teams, and the amazing players that had come through the program. I had never considered volleyball to be my dominant sport up until that point in my athletic career, but the thrill of being on such a successful team was something any competitive athlete would like to have been a part of. To be honest, being one of three freshmen to be on varsity, even if I wasn't a full-time player, was still quite intimidating that year, but thankfully, I had some incredible senior teammates that took me under their wing that season to really show me the ropes.

For drill after drill each practice, Coach Kim worked us hard and emphasized the "fake it until you feel it" concept. As a bunch of teenage girls with school, friend/boy drama, and more going on, that wasn't always as easy as it sounds, but that mentality on the court kept us solid and working as one. We were determined and we were good, and this was the year to make school history with three straight state championships. Our goals were written in our pre-season goal journals, and the rest of the state knew our aspirations as well.

Swinging for the first quarter of the season, my chance to step on the varsity court finally came. During our home tournament, one of our starting sophomore outside hitters took a nasty hit to the head, leaving her with concussion symptoms and me with a new starting position for the rest of the tournament. I played hard, and although inexperienced at that level of play, I played well. I found confidence in my ability to pull my own weight for the team. But even though I found confidence, all possible pride was stripped away when during one of the last games of our tournament, I ran off the court after serving because I was choking on my gum. Embarrassing, I know.

As the season progressed I eventually earned shared starting time with the sophomore outside hitter, but I desperately wanted to be the sole starter. Every practice,

I made a point to hustle more and try to just plain out-play her. I was going to earn that position.

Not until the end of the season at the state tournament did my hard work pay off. Just before the state tournament, I was made the starter.

It was the first round of the state championships. We were up against the highly ranked Corbett Cardinals, who had a powerful outside hitter and scrappy defense. We had prepared all week to combat them. From the start, it was hard to gain momentum for either team. Game after game, the scores were neck and neck. Game five rolled around, and it felt like we had everything to lose.

They would serve, and then we would serve. Back and forth. Back and forth. Neck and neck again. It was a fight, and us Eagles started to get a little frustrated with each other. Unity started to fall at that point. Finally, Corbett got a one point lead with one more point to finish the game. Our fight was gone, and efforts were exhausted. Then Corbett finished it. Our goal vanished. Exhausted and defeated, I watched as my senior team members fell to the ground in disappointment and exasperation. I saw one of my role models embrace her dad and bawl, as a dream to make school history had just been crushed. That was one of the most awful feelings I ever experienced. I personally hate the feeling of letting people down or disappointing them, and in that moment, I felt as if I had let down the entire team and dashed the goals of my senior leaders. We were out of the race for first, and it was devastating. The whole state was stunned that year, but we ended up taking fourth in state that season. At the end of that season, us returners vowed to one another, "Never again." We were going to make that history mark while we had the chance.

That following season, we not only wrote down our dreams of winning another state championship, but I personally wrote down my aspirations to make school history with three straight championships for the rest of my high school volleyball career. That was the dream, and I was going after it.

Looking back at these dreams of mine, I am so thankful that my parents always let me dream and didn't ever discourage it. Well, to a certain extent. As long as it didn't use their backyard as a breeding business for puppies. Let's be real, they probably would end up caring for my puppies. But beyond this, they always encouraged me to dream high and wide. I never felt any shackles or limits on what I could achieve. They always encouraged me to set goals for myself and make sure those goals were written down, recorded, and tracked. When I went after various goals, my parents always reinforced my drive with encouragement and participation. My dad would spend hours with me for volleyball working on my passing and hitting skills or helping perfect my shot in basketball. I think, too often, adults who have been through difficult times, especially parents that have endured medical tribulations, also forget to dream, and this trickles down to the limits they put on their kids. When a child has endured and overcome so much already, they have had to grow up faster than other children. But they need to keep dreaming! Dreaming reinforces victory in our lives. It is a sense of hope and of the promises of God's goodness. God has placed dreams in each of our hearts, big and small, child and adult. We are all dreamers, but it is your choice to capitalize on those dreams. You are never too old. Choosing victory every day means choosing to dream. It first happens by writing it down and making a commitment to it, like my teammates and I did after our state loss my freshman year. The next step is truly putting in the work to accomplish it. Whether that's saving for a goal or trip, training for an upcoming season, interviewing a person that has done a similar feat, or just doing some online research, it starts with taking action. So take action. Build a savings plan, create a training schedule, set that coffee date, or look it up. It's *your* time to dream!

Taking your pen and workbook, I want you to do some dream brainstorming. This is a process, so you don't have to have it all figured out, but you can use the

Victorious Workbook or your own notebook to start brainstorming dreams in these 12 areas of life: physical, emotional, intellectual, spiritual, psychological, material, professional, financial, creative, adventures, legacy, and character.

Now, as you determine each dream in these categories, I want you to list out at least two action steps on each. Lastly, on your worksheet, I want you to envision what life would look like if you were to reach each dream. As I have found in my athletic career, visualization of your dreams and the desired outcome is *huge* in preparing your mind to achieve that goal. Close your eyes, put on some music, and just think. What are those dreams in your heart? The things you would like to accomplish, see, feel, and experience in your lifetime. Some of these items may feel more like bucket list items, and others may resemble more direct goals. That is the fun in dreaming! Maybe they are places to travel, fitness goals to achieve, financial factors you are striving toward, or career opportunities you are chasing. The outcomes you are wanting are life-changing. Maybe achieving that fitness goal will help improve your overall energy levels and because of that you have more energy to devote to loved ones or doing another activity you love! That's awesome! These dreams you list are unique to you, and even though the future may seem far off and uncertain, it is *so* important you take this time to dream! Like I said earlier, it's your time to dream, friend.

Now that you have defined the dreams that are in your heart, it's time to act on those dreams. It's time to put the necessary steps in place to get you from where you are to where you want to be, and I am going to show you what that looks like and how you can track those dream accomplishments along the way.

*Chapter 10*

—◦◦◦◦◦◦◦—

# MEETING GOD HALFWAY

ou've established the dreams you are going after. I am so proud of you! And now it's time to put those action steps you listed out into action. It's easy to sit back and just dream and visualize outcomes, but our dreams still require some work on your part. It's what I have referred to in my own life as the "Meeting God Halfway" concept.

I learned this concept from the movie *Where the Red Fern Grows* in a conversation between the characters, Grandpa and Billy: "And if you want them bad enough, you'll get them, Billy. And if you want God's help bad enough, you'll meet him halfway."[11] I've learned that this goes for all of the dreams God has placed in our hearts. We still have to do some of the legwork, and God will do the rest. We cannot sit back and expect that God is just going to give us our dreams. Of course, prayer is always a component of meeting God halfway, but you need to put in the hard work of engaging and preparing for your dream journey. God has given you these dreams that pull on your heart for a reason, so in your efforts and training, God will reward and bless the endeavors you have put forth. He will open doors, provide favor, and give you the energy to keep moving forward.

After my defibrillation experience, getting back into the training of sports took some time, and, boy, it was not easy. There were not only physical barriers I had to overcome during my recovery, but there were mental barriers fresh in my mind—and these were uphill battles. Like I mentioned in previous chapters, it was difficult for me to even step foot on a basketball court even weeks after the experience. At times, it felt scary to exercise and to feel my heart rate increase even when I knew that my tachycardia had been taken care of during my last surgery. It wasn't easy, but I (with my

---

[11] *Where the Red Fern Grows* (Crown International Pictures, 1974).

victory tribe's help) kept going, and over time, it got easier. Up until that experience, my true sports passion was basketball, but after that basketball season, the game was never the same for me. At that point in my high school career, I became more focused on my volleyball career and going after that state championship dream I was chasing.

The spring following my freshman year of basketball, I started new training with weight lifting and agility. I started this workout regimen with a close family friend, Lance, who offered to train me and help me become a stronger all-around athlete because at that point in my athletic career, I was basically just athletic by nature and talent. I had not lifted weights or really trained outside the volleyball court, and I knew if I wanted to go after that state championship dream, it was time to get serious.

As I trained with Lance, I became stronger, more dynamic, and more powerful as an athlete. My confidence in my ability grew immensely, and it seemed to be a turning point in my athletic life. I was jumping higher, growing faster, and actually starting to feel as if I could really compete with the upperclassmen on my athletic teams.

The next volleyball season rolled around that fall before I knew it, and us returners from the previous Eagle team were on a mission to get that state title we had strived for the previous season. It was redemption time. From open gyms to camps that summer before the season, we trained with one mission: train to win. I still have a shirt that says that slogan from the season. Attending a retreat in Sunriver, Oregon, we truly got to know one another as teammates. I cannot quite explain what happened, but that summer, our quest to win and to truly be a united team shaped an incredible bond between all of us girls.

Not only were we friends on the court, but we also had a friendship off the court. That was a team I will never forget. Sure, there were times when we would get catty at each other and maybe lash out at one another in times of frustration, but regardless, we were one. We faked it until we felt it, even if that was on the court, and by the end, boy, did we feel it. Every drill was intentional as we worked for countless hours on our ball control in serve receive and serving. I also spent many hours outside and on the court with my dad sprinting, improving my footwork with jump roping, digging his hits, and practicing my hitting. Each rep, I trained with a purpose. Before every game, we had time in the locker room to visualize the game before us. Coach Kim would guide us through a visualization practice of envisioning the perfect pass, the perfect hit, the perfect execution of every play. This became a pre-game ritual for me no matter if Coach Kim guided us through it herself or if it was on my own. That was part of the hard work that going after my dream required. Not only was there physical preparation that needed to be completed, but I also needed to prepare myself mentally. That in itself was a task, but through strategic visualization, I was able to focus on each game at hand.

I think that people often underestimate the power of visualization in one's journey to achieving their dreams. I believe it is just as important to build up your mental acumen as it is your physical actions, because in all reality, the victory of your dreams starts in your thoughts. One of my favorite podcasts to listen to is the *Brian Buffini Show*, and one of my all-time favorite episodes is one where Buffini interviews Dick Hoyt, the father of Rick Hoyt, who has cerebral palsy.[12] Dick is famous for competing in athletic endeavors like marathons and Ironman triathlons where he would push Rick in his wheelchair, carry him in a special seat in front of a bicycle, or pull him in a special boat during competitions. Together Dick and Rick successfully competed in these competitions, and truly inspired so many with their grit, perseverance, and tenacity. In Buffini's interview with Dick, Buffini asks him how he was able to do such

---

[12]  The Brian Buffini Show, *The Brian Buffini Show*, April 20, 2021, https://www.thebrianbuffinishow.com/overcoming-adversity-an-interview-with-dick-hoyt-274/.

amazing feats. Dick promptly replies, "I just made up my mind." Now, if that doesn't speak volumes to the mental preparation that is needed to reach your dreams, I don't know what does. You have to not only put in the work physically, but you have to make up your mind.

Finishing league play and moving on to state, our volleyball team glided through the first round. Our hard work was paying off. The next wins also came pretty easily, and we found ourselves headed to the championship. And can you guess our opponent? You guessed it. Corbett. This was the time for redemption. What had been taken from us the year before was ours to claim that night. We had made up our minds.

Sitting in the hotel conference room before the match, my stomach was in knots. I had never been so nervous in my life for a game. It was so much more than a game to me at this point. It was a statement of deliberate hard work and perseverance, especially after the previous year's events.

The game began with a rapid start, and we pulled ahead with a 6 to 1 lead early in the first match. Everyone and every play was clicking. From each beautiful serve-receive pass, to the set, to the kill, our movements were precise. The momentum was ours. The entire first set, the Corbett Cardinals did not act as much of a threat as we kept the lead.

The second game approached and Corbett began with an 11 to 8 lead, but not for long. We knew how to battle. Kim called a time-out to give us a moment to breathe, and then we were off to the races. The score became 13 to 12. We then shortly regained the lead with a five-point consecutive streak, winning the second set of the volleyball game.

Into the final set of the game we went. This was our time. We all knew what the goal was, and we weren't backing down. We started the game with a 3 to 0 lead, and never looked back. I can still see our crowd raising their pointer fingers into the air symbolizing one more point to go to seal the deal as the score was 24-10, us.

Next thing I knew, the ball was being set outside for me to fulfill that one point everyone was expecting. And that last point was all mine.

As soon as my hit struck the ground, we were Champions. Mission accomplished.

There is definitely something to say about a championship feeling. There is nothing like it. It's as if your world has been paused for a moment, and an overwhelming feeling of satisfaction and joy takes over. Those countless hours in the gym, training for that goal despite the odds, setbacks, and discouragements had paid off. A dream was achieved. That medal hanging on my neck symbolized the feat, and for years afterward, acted as a reminder of the victory.

What have you been doing to prepare for your dreams? Do you know what is required to get there? Are you putting yourself in a position to reach them? If there's anything I've learned, it's that meeting God halfway requires consistency, and consistency breeds the wins you are looking for. When you have a chronic illness, it may require even more hard work. I know in my case, it took longer for me to get into shape, so those extra sessions outside of the gym were necessary to get into the shape I desired and fine-tune my skills. And that's okay! Even if it requires a lot of hard work, physically or mentally, you have to trust the process.

When you are in the training process and working to meet God halfway, it's important to track the dreams you have accomplished. Small and big! When you track your dreams, the achieved dreams serve as a reminder of what you have overcome by meeting God halfway. Just like the medal I received after winning that state championship was a reminder of the victory I had experienced that night, you need to have visual reminders of your dreams too. They are your victories to celebrate and remember! Personally, I track my dreams in a dream journal, and I use a special charm bracelet for my visual reminder of the dreams I have achieved. I got the idea for a dream bracelet when I saw my medals from high school dangling in my old bedroom. I wanted something bigger than just a journal where my dreams were written down. I wanted to wear my victories. So I purchased a Pandora bracelet, and every time I write down a dream I want to accomplish, I pick out the charm I will buy when I achieve that dream. So far, I have charms for becoming a wife, getting our first dog, buying our first house, and I know once this book gets published, I will have another charm to add to the bracelet. For me, this bracelet is a visual reminder of God's goodness and the blessings in my life as well. I have been given victory in my own life, and I get to wear those victories each and every day as my reminder to keep dreaming and going after God's promises, those dreams He has placed in my heart.

Tracking your dreams looks different for everyone, and it is up to you what makes it the most impactful experience for you. Maybe you are like me and you want more of a visual representation of your dreams; a dream bracelet may be the perfect option for you. However, a simple journal may be all you need to track your dreams and your progress toward them. I have seen people set rewards for every dream they achieve, like a special trip or buying themselves a pair of new running shoes. It's totally up to you!

Starting today, let's meet God halfway! To help you do this, I want you to do something for me. I want you to make a commitment. Using your Victorious Workbook or your notebook, I want you to write out your commitment to meeting God halfway while going after your dreams. Now, I want you to email that commitment to me at victorious@torijoygeiger.com. This action of emailing will signify you are making up your mind.

Now that you've made up your mind, you are ready to get after it! I'll be honest. It isn't the instant gratification that we all desire most of the time, but over time, you will get to that dream because you have made up your mind and are putting in the necessary actions. I believe God honors that. I have seen it in my own life, and I know you will too. The consistency you are practicing requires patience and the ability to trust the process, and in that waiting, the greatest blessings occur.

*Chapter 11*

———⟨∼⟩———

# IN THE WAITING

*I* don't know about you, but I have a hard time with patience. It's not that I am an extremely impatient person, but more that I tend to rush through life trying to get to the next thing. This makes it hard to truly embrace the "moment." That's why when I set a dream I want to achieve, I sometimes have the hardest time being patient for its arrival. It's not easy.

A year or so ago, I was listening to a podcast where the host interviewed a fellow CHD friend of mine who is a bit older than me. In her interview, she mentioned something that truly resonated with me. She explained that she felt as if she was always rushing through life from fear of missing out. She felt like she had to just keep plowing ahead, and what she realized was that she felt this way because of her chronic illness. She felt like she had to "get it all done" because she didn't know when the next thing would appear related to her chronic illness.[13] Wow. That *hit* me. That was so me. And to be totally transparent, it's still something I battle with mentally. Especially after that defibrillation event, I felt like I had to accomplish everything on my bucket list as soon as possible. And while I have achieved a lot of great things in my 23 years of living, from state championships, to awards, to successful businesses, I had the hardest time focusing on the here and now. Over the years, I have felt the effects of this "rushing." It inhibited my relationships, and put a lot of stress and unneeded pressure on myself. The worst part for me was that this "rushing" was so subconscious, I didn't even realize I was doing it for years. It took time for me to admit that it was a problem for me.

Maybe you don't realize that this is something you have felt or are currently feeling. That's okay! That's normal. I have been right where you are. You may be an Enneagram 3 like me, and think that it is just part of your personality, but I would make sure to evaluate if there may be more to your "busyness" and desire to

---

[13]    Navigating The True North, *Navigating The True North*, September 24, 2019, https://podcasts.apple.com/pl/podcast/navigating-the-true-north/id1469489916.

achieve the next thing in life. You could be a victim of the same subconscious thoughts I discovered.

While you are waiting for your dreams to come to fruition, it is easy to rush through the rest of life and not embrace the here and now. I know in America, it's a little bit baked into the culture we live in, especially in the business culture I've been around. But let me tell you, it's the moments in between achieving those dreams that you will want to remember just as well as the accomplishment of the dreams. You may be in the stage of life where you are waiting. You are being consistent, putting in the work, but you are still waiting and trusting for those dreams and goals to come to fruition. I know it's hard, but in this patience, that is when God places people in your life, opportunities, and blessings that you are sure to miss out on if you keep rushing through life trying to get to the next achievement, the next surgery, the next prognosis. You are just living to survive, not thrive. When you embrace the waiting and acknowledge that you are in a time that requires patience, the power is back in your hands. There are many ways to acknowledge patience in your life, and one way I have found helpful is through prayer and affirmations. These prayers and affirmations help slow me down when I get into frustrated, inpatient, "rushing Tori" mode and remind me to embrace the patience that is required as I trust the process.

I am going to share these affirmations with you as well! Repeat these after me.

"I am deserving of the dreams God has given me."

"I know that I am in a waiting period in my life where I must be patient."

"I embrace each moment rather than rush through life to get to the next thing because I will be blessed in the waiting."

"Busyness will not get the best of me as I go after my dreams."

"My dreams are right in front of me, and I trust the process to get there."

Below is a little prayer that I say when the waiting gets *really* tough. It's the commitment I have made between God and myself to trust him as I put in the work. If you feel so led, you can pray this prayer too.

"God, I am going to meet you halfway. These are dreams you have orchestrated in my life. I will put my best effort into growing and preparing for my dreams. Show me the direction, and I will walk toward it. Give me the strength to persevere for my dreams even when it gets hard because I know your hand is there to guide me. With you, my dreams are possible."

Wow. Doesn't that feel good?

Does a weight feel like it's been lifted?

Good!

Developing this mindset during those times of waiting builds resiliency. By remembering to embrace each moment rather than rush to the next thing, we are able to be more flexible and adaptable when our plans in life change. And we know, as survivors of chronic illnesses, we have to quickly learn how to change our course of action when your world is turned upside down. Being a survivor of a chronic illness makes you pretty adaptable to begin with, but by developing this patience, you are ready to easily change your course of action when needed. Ultimately, you are better prepared to flip the script and go after the new opportunities presented when you are directed into a change of plans.

*Chapter 12*

---

# FLIP THE SCRIPT

You've set goals. You've dreamed big dreams. You've put in the consistent work to get there. That is awesome! But in one moment, those plans can change.

As you've probably discovered, life doesn't really happen in a linear fashion. Sometimes there is a lot of weaving in and out along a path while we discover and learn more in this life. And I know we've all been there experiencing those negative and/or positive moments that change the course of our expectations. To be frank, it's bound to happen to you no matter if you have a chronic illness or not. It is the steps you take during those detours that keep you on the path to living a victorious life even if it doesn't look exactly how you originally pictured.

I personally am a planner by nature, and I have a really hard time when things go "off plan." And I will say, my script has been flipped many times throughout my life, but in every way, there has no doubt been even bigger blessings in those circumstances. Those "change of plans" have been moments that have truly helped shape me as a person.

I had just begun dating my junior high crush for only a couple of months when the reality of my heart condition really slapped me in the face. It was young love. Or, well, "in love" as much as you could as a freshman in high school. This being my first real boyfriend, everything was so exciting, and the future seemed so enthralling. One day, I was sitting with my mom just talking about how much I loved this relationship I was in and the future we could have. I mean, we were perfect for each other, or so I thought at that time in my life. Somehow, as my mom and I began discussing the future, we started talking about kids. I remember going on and on to her about how much fun it will be to be a mom someday and how excited I was to one day have a mini-me running around. That's when reality hit. After I ecstatically explained those dreams I had, my mom softly explained to me that I was at the age where she should tell me some of the conversations that the doctors had had with them over the years. She explained that having children down the line may not be a possibility for me due to my heart's complications and the stress a pregnancy could cause. At that time in my life, it was assumed by the doctors that adoption or surrogacy would be my options due to the many unknowns with my heart. Hearing that news was a major shock to me. I guess I had never truly thought about that impossibility. I had just thought that part of me would be like everyone else.

If anything, that news was a blow to my confidence. As a young girl who had just started dating, it really challenged my worth as a woman. I definitely had thoughts like, *If I can't give the person I love children, am I worth staying with?* The happy plans and future family I saw for myself seemed to take a turn so quickly.

If there is anything I have learned over the years as I have set goals, gone after dreams, or had a particular vision for my life, it is that your plans *will* evolve. Sometimes those plans can be an exciting new opportunity that you didn't see coming, but other times those new plans are less than wonderful. That change in plan could be a new diagnosis or the loss of an ability to do something you love or desired. It is by no means an easy thing to process.

Processing that new direction in your life definitely takes some time. But, over the years, as my plans have evolved, I have learned a process that helps me deal and adapt to the evolving dream or detour I am on.

First, you have to grieve. What I mean by this is that you have to take time to process the loss of what you thought your life would be like and the dreams that came along with that vision. This grieving process is perfectly normal. It helps you come to terms with the reality you are facing. I think, too often, when we receive bad news or have a traumatic event, we are taught to have a false positivity mindset or what I call "toxic positivity." Toxic positivity means to "just think about good vibes" or only focus on the positive without acknowledging the true reality of our circumstances. This does nothing but mask the emotions of loss and discouragement you are feeling inside, and those emotions cannot be masked forever. It is *way* better to take the time to express those emotions, whether that be with a close friend, family member, journaling, or a therapist. For me, it took a lot of my high school years and early college years to come to terms with the reality of not having children through my own pregnancy—if that indeed came true. I highly encourage you to take the time to talk through and process the dreams or plans you are laying to rest. Like in my case, it took years to fully process the reality of my heart condition. And that is okay! Take your time! It is so important to do this because you must grieve first to move along in your journey of victory through your chronic illness battle.

Now that you have acknowledged those losses, you need to reclaim yourself. With that feeling of loss and the change of plans, we often "lose" who we truly are. Our identity often becomes wrapped up in the dreams we have set for ourselves or the life we have envisioned, and when those things don't come to fruition, we feel like we have lost a piece of ourselves. This happened to me several times, like after that traumatic basketball game where my athletic career was up in the air and when my worth felt challenged by the potential to not be able to bear children. In those moments, it is most important to dig into who we really are. We must reclaim that person! And I am not saying things like, "I am a volleyball player" or "world traveler" or "fashion model." I am talking about who we are at our *core*. I am saying things like:

"I am a true friend."

"I have grit."

"I am kind."

"I am brave."

"I am worthy and enough."

"I am loved."

"I am a daughter of Christ."

These are things that I journal during this process as I return to who I truly am at my core. You can even have others chime in during this process. Ask your friend or family member, "Who am I at my core?" or

"When am I my best self?" This can help get you started as you journal about your true self. In this step, you are reaffirming the true strength you have even when you feel weak in that moment after suffering a loss of your future plans. By journaling about who you are, you are exhibiting your power in your circumstances by putting that pen to paper. You are also setting a foundation for yourself to return to in the future when you are facing other adversities.

When I am having an off day, I love reading back through journal entries or notes from friends and remembering that core of who I am because, in the chaos and adversity, it is so easy to forget. It is also so crazy to see the growth I have experienced as a person while the core of who I am has stayed the same over the years. After all, you are *not* defined by these detours to your plans. Rather, they are shaping you to become the best version of yourself at your core.

Once you have reclaimed who you are at your core, it is time to flip the script. It's your time to use this change of plans in your life to fuel your victory story. You are ready to look for blessings in the new journey you are on and continue to dream once again. It may be scary to dream again after the dreams you thought you had have been disrupted, but it is an important part of the process. For me, I found blessings in the fact that I was able to rediscover my worth as a woman during that time in my life, and also realize that my worth wasn't lessened by my ability to give my future spouse children—or my ability to do anything, for that matter. My worth was in being a daughter of Christ who is strong, worthy, and capable to achieve great things no matter my circumstances. I cannot even explain how much I immensely grew from that clarity in all areas of my life, from personal to professional. It built my confidence like no achievement or accolade could. I was able to flip the script of those changed plans by better defining who I was as a person and where my worth was derived from. Rather than letting those possible limitations define me and keep me stagnant, I refused to let those new circumstances keep me from dreaming. Instead, I set other dreams for myself and just kept moving forward.

That's what you need to do too. You need to look for the blessings in this new journey. Start by considering what you might be learning about yourself or about how to handle a circumstance. Maybe you are learning to be more assertive with doctors or slowing down in life. That is great! There is always something to learn when our plans change.

After you have spent some time considering the things you are learning, it's time to put some new dreams down on paper. Now, I know you previously filled out your dreams in Chapter 9's section of the workbook, so I am just going to give you some affirmations to write down in this section of the workbook as a reminder to keep dreaming even when your directions change.

Affirmations:

"I am adaptable even when my plans change. After all, my dreams are there to help me grow to be the best I can be."

"I am not perfect, and neither are my plans. Therefore, I will continue to look for the blessings in every direction life takes me."

I am so excited for you to be able to utilize this three-step process that I have found so helpful over the years as I have grieved the loss of dreams and continued to grow and move forward. It's in that process where we are able to truly flip our script and use the change in circumstances to better ourselves and our future. Sometimes when you least expect it, that change of plan can actually be the catalyst that leads you to greater victories than you thought possible.

# Chapter 13

## FROM UNDERDOG TO JUGGERNAUT

When your plans change, and then you begin dreaming again, you start back at ground zero. It's the underdog position. And in my opinion, that's the best spot. Well, at least it's the most exciting position to be in. When you have been knocked down from the dreams you were going after, it's a time where many people in your life may underestimate you. But when you have been able to adapt to your change of direction and find the growth in that learning experience, you are building a resiliency that turns you into a force to be reckoned with. In other words, a juggernaut.

The next volleyball season was our year to repeat our previous volleyball victory and achieve back-to-back state titles. After our championship win the previous year, spectators across our state division believed that we had lost too much talent to stay at the top. They believed it was the end of our championship dynasty.

At the beginning of the season, our team entered highly competitive tournaments outside of our regular league play. This allowed us to get more experience with tougher opponents that were not in our 3A state division. In those extra tournaments, we were competing against some of the toughest teams in the state that were in higher divisions and stacked with some of the best players across the state and in some cases, even nationally. And the best part? We were winning those tough tournaments. We put every effort into these games, and played fearlessly no matter the opponent. Walking away from one of the biggest tournaments we played in that year, us SC Eagles took down the defending 5A champions (two divisions above us) and claimed the championship of the *entire* tournament. From that tournament win in particular, we had sent out a message to the spectators in our state division. Santiam Christian was the team to beat, once again. That's when our team was termed the "juggernaut" in our local paper. Ever since then, I've just loved that word.

We held to that juggernaut image after that tournament win and all of the regular season. We never lost it. After qualifying for our division's state tournament that year, we made it once again to the state championship for the second year in a row. That year, we achieved the back to back state championship we had set our eyes on. Us, SC Eagles were State champions once again!

Senior season for volleyball the next fall arrived faster than I anticipated, and this was the year we could attempt three back to back state championships, a big high school dream of mine. We had failed in this attempt my freshman year of high school, and this memory was looming in our minds as we trained for the upcoming season. This year, the state *really did* doubt our abilities as we had now lost half of our key starters which was a lot more talent than we had lost the previous year.

That year, we had three very talented but inexperienced freshmen that filled those vacant roles on our team, and all eyes were on our senior leadership to see if we could pull another championship off. Because of the major underestimation, senior year had to be my favorite season of all time. It was a year with the most doubts, most leadership needs, and most incredible championship experience.

At the beginning of the season, we seniors took it upon our shoulders to help our new freshmen teammates feel like a part of our team. We had pancake feeds in addition to morning workouts before our summer training camp sessions. We did our best to show the younger classmen the ropes and explain the expectation and preparation needed to win the championship we were after. Additionally, with the news of it also being Coach Kim's final year, we felt this was the year to make the most of. During our practices, if we made errors during drills and plays, we did short sprints in sets of 10 as discipline. I remember one practice not long before playoffs that we were all dragging, and the coaches were not at practice at that moment. We messed up on a ball control drill that required us to get so many controlled rallies before we could end the drill, and we did not reach that requirement. Some of my teammates laughingly said, "Well, coaches aren't here. Let's just start over and try again."

With that comment, I can still see us seniors glancing at each other, all thinking the same thing.

I replied to our teammates, "I do not want to get to the championship game and lose because we are exhausted or not in good enough shape. That will not be the reason that we lose, so we are going to do the lines no matter how tired we are and no matter who is watching."

Boy, did I not anticipate how needed those reps were going to be later in the season.

After league play, the state finals rolled around quickly as they did the previous years, and we were all nervous, including us seasoned veterans. We walked into the state tournament gym with what Coach Kim referred to as a "cocky confidence" but with the fear of God under us too. The pressure was on.

The first round of the state playoff tournament kicked off in the early morning, and it was a rough one. The pressure and nerves really got into my head and threw my game off. Error after error I made, it felt like I could see the win slipping away.

But not for long.

My teammates were right there picking up the extra weight of my errors play after play as we fought as a team. We miraculously pulled off our first victory of the tournament. We were safe and on to the next round that would take place later that evening.

Even though we won, I was still worried about my performance as a leader on the team. I could not make that many errors and expect to somehow pull off a win in the games to come. I had to get focused. Once we returned to our hotel, I put my headphones on to visualize each skill perfectly. Every serve. Every pass. Every hit, block, tip, you name it. I beat my opponent flawlessly every play. I had trained for this. I was now ready.

This visualization and focus apparently did come together as we headed into our next game that evening. We came out with an easy win.

Next stop, championship. We made it. This was it. Our dream was within grasp. We didn't have a doubt in our minds that that championship was ours to claim. But unlike most other games we had faced all season, it was going to be a tough fight.

Earlier that week before our team had headed off to Eugene, Oregon, to stay down there for that championship weekend, we had been doing some serve-receive passing with our mechanical serving machine to simulate some of the toughest serves we would face during the tournament. One particular play, I turned my head to reach down and grab a volleyball near the court when I was struck in the side of the head by one of the machine-served balls, leaving me with a little bit of a headache. I just shook the headache off and kept playing, not thinking much of it. I had little headaches throughout the week, but I didn't even stop long enough that week to consider them. All my mind was focused on was the state tournament and title at hand.

It was the championship. Saturday night, November 8, 2014. Our opponent, Creswell, was a talented team to beat. Similar to Corbett, the team we had faced my freshman and sophomore year, Creswell was scrappy, and had a couple power hitters that were threats. We all knew it was going to be a challenge.

Winning the first set, we felt confident in our performance. Then the second set rolled around and error after error began to separate us from our desired lead.

It wasn't until the second game of the championship that that previous week's head injury became a little more apparent. Diving for a ball while covering the outside hitter, I took a knee to the opposite temple that was hit at practice earlier in the week.

My head was pounding after that, and at almost every time-out, I was at the trashcan gagging. Honestly, I thought I was just nervous for the game. But that was just the start of it.

We dropped the second and third set, and at that point, we were all in question of our defending title aspirations. What was happening out there?

I remember Coach Kim reminding us to dig deep and fight it out. Loaded with ibuprofen and Gatorade, I played on. We went into set four narrowly winning 25 to 23 and tying up the sets as we headed into the fifth and final set of the game. It was all on the line now.

Neck and neck from the start of the set, we just kept fighting. I was exhausted and gagging as I transitioned between every play. It was awful.

"Guys, I need you to really step up right now," I told the freshmen. "Let's do this."

And, boy, did everyone fight, especially those freshmen. Those lines during practices were really paying off. More than we ever thought they would.

The score was now 14 to 13, with Creswell in the lead, when I came to serve with the game point looming. There could be no errors made by us Eagles. After my serve, the ball was returned by Creswell, but only to be finished off by a powerful kill from my teammate, Katy Paratore. The score then rested at 14 to 14, giving us a little more peace after that nerve-racking serve. My next serve was almost returned by Creswell, only to be quickly blocked by us Eagles, leaving the score at 15 to 14. After a couple more rallies and errors by our team, Creswell was able to catch our lead, still giving us a hard-fought battle. Still maintaining the lead at 17 to 16, us Eagles were clinging on. With my freshman teammate, Leah Boyer, up to serve for game point, the pressure was even more immense. One more point to seal the deal. Leah served the ball perfectly, and Creswell made the attempt to return the ball on a kill from the middle. I remember that play like none other. It felt like slow motion as Creswell's hitter went up to attack the ball. I remember watching the ball in the air after it left her hand and chasing it all the way to the back line as everyone screamed "OUT!" After it hit the ground untouched by us Eagles and the referee's flag shot up in the air symbolizing "out of bounds," we all stared at each other for what felt like minutes. And it hit us. We proceeded to run to each other screaming in victory as our student section stormed the court. We did it. School history was made. It was time to celebrate!

I did not get to celebrate this victory for too long, as my head caught up with me after the adrenaline wore off, and, boy, was that painful. I recovered after a couple weeks from a concussion, and I am still shocked I was able to perform that game. I mean, 31 kills with a concussion is pretty neat, but I would not recommend that for any healthy athlete. I guess this was *another* lesson in listening to my body.

I learned so much about what it is like to be underestimated, especially by everyone around you. Whether that was on the volleyball court or in the hospital room. When our plans have been shaken up or our circumstances have changed, typically that's when there is the most doubt in our lives and the most underestimation. But the exciting thing is we can use that underestimation to fuel our victory and become that juggernaut I talked about. And through that fuel, we can surprise people around us, the people that underestimate us. We can surprise our friends, family, and even doctors in how we are still moving forward. People are looking to see, "Will she bounce back?" "How is she going to handle this circumstance?" And when you do keep moving forward, your victory will inspire everyone around you. I am not saying that your motive to keep moving forward is to surprise people or "prove them wrong," but I want you to know that surprise and inspiration is a byproduct of choosing to express gratitude, working hard toward those dreams, and getting back up every time your chronic illness pushes you down. We all have the capabilities within us to be a juggernaut, even when living with a chronic illness, and we live into that capability by doing these things that lead to victory in our lives. We *are* a force to be reckoned with. Once you have achieved even the smallest of victories, it is also time to celebrate those feats!

Celebrating every milestone, every victory, big or small, is *huge*. Whether that is having a good day in a long time, a positive hospital visit, or a new skill learned, it needs to be celebrated because it is a victory in your story! The underestimation you have faced as a chronic illness warrior makes celebrating those victories even sweeter! You have to celebrate the victories like you've just won a championship, because you have, and you want to remember what it feels like to do so. Remembering that victory feeling is key when you are going through a current battle because it reminds you of the resilience you have within. It helps you recognize that strength and courage that can feel so distant when you are fighting so hard. For me, winning championships in high school was a great feat, but in all honesty, it wasn't about the athletic accolades. Those wins symbolized the victory I was having over my chronic illness. Instead of living in fear of many unknowns or in the paralysis of what happened at that scary basketball game, I was pouring myself into being the best I could be as a teammate and athlete. When I am going through difficult times with my CHD even now, I remember that championship victory feeling, and it reminds me of the strength and person it took to accomplish that victory.

Start planning those victory celebrations now so you are ready to party when you have experienced that victory! I am going to help you prepare for those celebrations. Using your Victorious Workbook or notebook, I want you to write down three different ways you can celebrate a victory. These can be as simple as going out for some ice cream with friends or going to your favorite place to visit. It is totally up to you. The key is to make it something memorable and something you enjoy. I still to this day go out for ice cream or a treat after every annual heart appointment to celebrate another year of victory in my heart journey. It's those little things, celebrating those wins, that add up to the greatest impact, in my opinion.

Isn't it fun to be the underdog? Well, I know I am excited to see all the things you are going to do as you show others the juggernaut you truly are! Keep celebrating your victories as they come, big and small, and as you do this, your victory story will keep building momentum. And as you gain momentum with your victories, you have the opportunity to use your story to inspire and empower others on the same journey as you.

# Chapter 19

—⁓∿∘᪣᪤᪥᪦ᪧ∘∿⁓—

# MAKE IT YOUR
# BATTLE CRY

*W*ell, you've achieved a victory in your journey and you've celebrated it. Congratulations! But what's next? Winning a championship or having a good doctor's appointment doesn't mean that your victory journey has come to a close. There will be more mountains you will have and most definitely more valleys, but you know what? You know what it takes to continue to live a life of victory no matter your circumstances. When you live in this way of victory, you are truly embodying the mindset that "the best is yet to come." I am not saying that you are not content in your current circumstances; I am just saying that when you have a mindset of "the best is yet to come," you are manifesting that truth into your life and pushing yourself to keep growing. If you keep growing, it is true that the best will continue to come!

Once the season ended and my head healed, I announced my commitment to attend Corban University and signed my letter of intent to play under Coach Kim, who had taken the position of head coach of the Corban Warriors. I was ecstatic to play under my high school coach and with some of my present and former high school teammates that upcoming year.

Fall camp approached, and the team was looking sharp. I felt stronger and more developed as a player. I enjoyed my teammates, the team atmosphere, and the hard work. Collegiate play was another world, and I loved it. Our team relationships continued to build during fall camp, and it was a whole new learning experience working with other personalities that I didn't grow up with and were different from other teammates I had played with in the past.

Before Coach Kim Mclain took over the Warrior program, the team had had some challenging losing seasons, and Kim was hired in anticipation of turning the program around and merging the existing team with new recruits. At the start of pre-season, we felt confident in our talent and skill as we headed into our first tournament in eastern Oregon. That tournament was a wake-up call for all of us. Losing every game, we headed home pretty discouraged. Personally, this one tournament was more losses than I had experienced in probably my whole volleyball career in high school. But it made me realize I was playing at a higher level, and I had to rise to that level of play if I wanted to succeed as I did in high school. It wasn't going to be as easy. Just as we did in high school, at our next practices we focused on our serve-receive passing, serving, and blocking, as those were our apparent weaknesses from the past games. Gradually, we started to work out the kinks.

School also began. As it was my first year of college, life became a very interesting dynamic. Thankfully high school taught me time management. That habit I developed helped me stay balanced as I attacked long practices and early-morning classes. I'm not saying staying organized gave me time because I hardly had minutes to spare during the day, but it helped keep my stress under control. When people say being a college athlete is a job, they are totally correct. It's a full-time job, but a fun one.

The season continued, and there were ups and downs along the way. Defeating College of Idaho at home was one of the best feelings, as our gym was packed and they were a nationally ranked team. I was a starter off and on throughout the season, as I became a better hitter. At one point late in the season, I carried a .500 hitting average against Northwest Christian University.

As the season drew on, though, I found myself struggling to really find my passion at Corban. Practices became longer, classes and activities were not as inviting, and I didn't feel the joy about attending Corban like I had when I committed originally. I did not see myself graduating from Corban or truly growing as I could elsewhere. It just didn't feel right for some reason. My heart was torn in two because I had built so many relationships, and the people at Corban were so genuine. But when it came down to it, Corban was just not the place I was supposed to be.

One of the hardest decisions and conversations I have ever had was telling Coach Kim that I was leaving Corban. I remember texting her, asking to meet with her after the season. I walked down the big hill at Corban to the sports office where she worked. That walk felt like the longest hike as I tried to gather the words I was going to say. We sat down, and the words just started flowing. I poured out my heart, explaining my passion for business and hopes for my career and that I did not see Corban as a part of it. Tears were shed from both of us as she encouraged me to pursue my passions and go after the future I wanted. She supported my decision to transfer to George Fox University, where my brother attended, and she graciously even offered to give an athletic recommendation if I decided to do athletics at Fox. However, after years of training pretty intensely for volleyball in high school and that one season at Corban, I felt like my life was needing a shift. In some ways, I felt like it was time to turn the page and start focusing on more of my career and business dreams rather than putting so much energy into athletics. At that point in time, I was pretty set on just focusing on school and "retiring" from competing collegiately.

Honestly, that conversation with Coach Kim was a blessing in my life. The words that were spoken did not really feel like my own. They felt guided by the Holy Spirit. God knew my heart towards turning the page in my life, and even though I didn't exactly know what the future held, I felt like God was right there in the room guiding me to take my next step. After my meeting with Coach Kim, I had closure and was ready to move on to my next adventure.

I genuinely believe that there was a reason for spending my first semester of college at Corban. It was supposed to be a part of my story. The incredible relationships I built with teammates are something I dearly treasure. Even after transferring to George Fox, I still maintained some of those friendships. One of my teammates was even my maid of honor in my wedding years later. I also believe that I needed some time to adjust to college and gain more confidence in myself as a student athlete, and my time at Corban allowed me to do that.

I was thrilled to be at Fox, and when I started the spring semester that January, I felt at home in Newberg. I began working at a job in the College of Business aside from classes, and tried to keep myself busy with business networking events, studying, and working. Although I thought that "turning the page" to the next chapter for me meant leaving college athletics behind, I really started missing the team atmosphere quite a lot, and my competitive cravings were killing me about the second month of being at Fox. Around that time, one of my brother's friends tried to talk me into going out for high jump on the women's track team since I was having those feelings. As I thought about it, going out for track looked like a way I could still stay in shape, and I could also meet more people since I was new to the University. I did have a *little* high jumping experience from one track season in high school, but I would hardly call that experience. I kind of shrugged off my brother's friend's suggestions at first, but I later sat down for a brief meeting with the track team's head coach, John, one day. He encouraged me to work out with the team and only compete if I really wanted to. I agreed to just work out and see how it went over the next few months.

Well, I guess you could say it went pretty well since I competed for four years on that team, won a conference title in the high jump, and was a part of multiple women's conference championships. Oh, and did I mention, I met my husband, Devin, there? That's a fun story for another time!

Some of my greatest victories and growth in college happened while I was on the track team, and if you would have told me in high school or even as I left Corban that I would be competing collegiately in track, I would have laughed at you. During my years as a track athlete, I had to learn to listen to my body even more since the training was more intense than I had ever experienced in my athletic career. I laugh at myself when I think about how I was joining the track team at first to "just work out." Boy, did I have no idea what was coming. As I left Corban, I thought that "turning the page" to my next chapter in life meant without college athletics because I wasn't continuing with volleyball, and I was pursuing some other dreams. But little did I know that there were still areas of my life I had to grow in for me to pursue those other dreams. And those areas of growth were to come from competing in track and field.

The mental toughness I had to learn in high jump was *very* significant in this growth I experienced as well. I mean, they literally move the bar up two inches from the previous bar you *just* cleared and somehow mentally that is one of the most challenging things! Track forced me to try something new without being afraid to fail.

Playing volleyball was safe, something I knew and I was good at. It was something I had already experienced victory in, but high jump was new territory.

I think when we are coming off of a "victory," or a mountaintop experience of achieving a goal or meeting a milestone, we are often scared to keep moving forward because we want that "championship" feeling to last. In reality, it is more a fear of failing or having to struggle again after we have achieved that victory. I totally get it. It's happened for me in athletics, in college, and especially as a heart patient. I still get a little bit of that pre-anxiety before doctor visits even though I have faith that everything will be fine. That's our human reaction. Let's be honest, it's easy to maintain a victory mindset when you are living a victory. It's not so easy when you go from mountaintop to valley. That is why it is so important to lean into your past to keep propelling you toward your future. Now, I am not saying to keep living in the past, but I am saying to use those past experiences to keep fueling you to move forward. I tell people, use your experiences with your chronic illness as your battle cry! Whether you are on the mountaintop or in the valley, those experiences serve as a reminder of what you have overcome, what has made you so incredible, and what helps you continue to relate and care for others going through similar journeys. In that way, your battle cry is one of a survivor, mover, and shaker.

When you embrace this mentality, it is going to launch you through the valleys to new victories.

I want you to do something for me. I want you to write down your battle cry. Today. Using your Victorious Workbook, you can fill in the blanks of your battle cry statement, or you can make your own below. The fill-in-the-blank may be a great place to start, and you can craft it more and more to your liking! It's totally up to you!

It can go something like this:

"I am a survivor that has *overcome* a chronic illness all my life. I am stronger, more empathetic, and inspirational because of it."

Yes, friend! You are *living* with a chronic illness. Do you know how much guts, grit, and gumption (love that word) you have in order to live with something like that? A whole lot. You are an overcomer in more ways than you may realize. It's those battle scars that have turned into your battle cry. And it's now time to share the foundation of that battle cry with others that need to hear your story as well.

It's time to share your victory story.

*Chapter 15*

~~~~~~~~~~~~~~

# IT'S YOUR TIME TO INSPIRE

*D*id you know that there are so many people on this planet that need to hear your story? There are other individuals just like you that need the inspiration and perspective you bring. I've learned over the years that someone could hear an inspiring message thousands of times, but it takes that one person with a particular perspective or experience to really make it stick. Do you know what I mean? Have you ever had a teacher that you just cannot understand, but then you have a new teacher or tutor explain the same thing in a different way, and it seems so easy? It's just like that with your story. There is a lot of "noise" in our world today, but it takes one person's experience to inspire another person to keep fighting. You too can use your experiences to make an impact.

For some reason, as I grew up, I always felt some sort of special pull in my life. There had already been so much that had happened in my life from such an early age. You could call it a forced growing up. I was often referred to as a "miracle child" because of the complications of my arrival. I didn't truly understand what my parents and I had gone through until later in my elementary years, but still I loved telling people, "I have a big heart. Literally." I thought it made me look pretty cool. My name's meaning, "victorious," really rang true in my life, and God's guiding hand displayed through my name's meaning resulted in even more depth in my everyday life.

With so many individuals praying for me at an early age, many people were involved in my story from the beginning. Constantly, friends of my parents and grandparents told me, "I remember praying for you before you were born." I didn't even realize the impact of all these people until later in my life. Even in church, I was about the age of seven or eight when our pastor had me come to the front of the stage to tell my story. It was a fun experience having the opportunity to share my story. After this little segment with my pastor, more people from our church, even strangers, would come up to me and comment on my powerful story and how it inspired them. It was around then that I knew I wanted to someday write a book telling my story, and I didn't even know the things I would go through years later with my heart.

Over the years, I have gotten the opportunity to share my story with larger audiences, like during my high school's chapel, and every time I shared my story, more people were touched. When I hit my sophomore year of college, one of our business class assignments was to design a company and market it. As the leader of my group at the time, I decided our group would design an activewear company that gave part of its proceeds to CHD organizations. It was at that point in my life when I knew that I wanted to use my story and my business knowledge to make an impact. Now, that exact activewear company didn't come to fruition, but out of it, I discovered that calling in my life, and that has now turned into the lifestyle blog platform I have today called Tori Joy Geiger. Through this platform, I have been able to meet so many incredible other CHD'ers and parents of CHD'ers, which has been the most rewarding experience! I get to help provide hope, support, and friendship to others walking similar paths to mine.

One of the most inspiring stories I have ever heard belongs to a pro surfer girl by the name of Bethany Hamilton. Maybe you have heard of her too. Hamilton, at a young age, had her eyes set on a career as a surfing pro, but one particular surfing trip changed her forever when she was attacked by a shark. She lost an arm, and her dreams were seemingly dashed.

Later she went on to become a pro surfer anyway, write a book about her uphill battle, and even have a movie written about her story. My favorite quote of hers is, "I've had the chance to embrace more people with one arm than I ever could with two."[14]

Wow. That could not be more true. In my life, I feel the same way. My big heart has not only allowed me, but also my parents to encourage, inspire, and love so many more people than we ever would have without this story of mine. Having a big heart has given me more room in my heart for those people. Teammates', friends', even perfect strangers' lives have been influenced by God's hand in my story.

Humans are wired to send and receive narratives with each other. This is true from the beginning of time. I mean, look at how Jesus taught his disciples through parables. In the same way, God gives us these testimonies of our lives to have fellowship with one another and share hope and light with others. A huge part of claiming your victory over your chronic illness is by beginning to share your experiences with others.

---

[14]   *Soul Surfer* (TriStar Pictures, 2011).

Whether that is through writing a book, joining an online community, or just openly sharing your story with friends, family members, or co-workers, it's your time to share your story.

I personally felt called to go the self-publishing route, as it has always been a dream of mine to write this book. And, hey, if you want to write your story in a book like this one, I would *love* to read it. And I cannot recommend Self-Publishing School enough, the program I followed to self-publish this book. It is such a blessing to be coached and mentored throughout my authorship experience, and I could not be more grateful for this journey.

Now, some of your major life events may not be past ones but rather present storms you are struggling through on your chronic illness journey. Or you may be angry with God for current or past circumstances just as I was when my tachycardia returned. Do not worry. You can still share your story even in the midst of the storm. And you know what? Your story is even more powerful when you are sharing it as you weather the storm. One thing I have been really learning recently is that God speaks through our weaknesses. In our weakest times, that is when God uses us and our stories to make an impact on others. So just because you don't have it all figured out or you are struggling through some current storms, it doesn't mean you should refrain from sharing your amazing, resilient, story.

I also want to share with you two potential mindset traps that may keep you from sharing your story. I have battled both myself. Those traps are the "I'm the only one" mindset and Imposter Syndrome. Like the name suggests, the "I'm the only one" mindset happens when you think you are the only one going through a certain trial and that no one can relate to what you are going through. Imposter Syndrome is basically when you feel like you aren't qualified enough or have a sense that you haven't earned what you've achieved, making you feel like a fraud when you share your experience.

Let me stomp a bit on both of these syndromes. Do not believe them! Don't fall captive to these syndromes! I know at times I had thoughts like, *No one can relate to what I am feeling,* and *My story isn't as rough or traumatic as theirs, so it isn't as inspiring.* First of all, your story is unique because it's *your* story, and because you have weathered the storms of living with a chronic illness, you are insanely qualified to speak on *your* experience. Don't ever let anyone tell you differently. Do not let the comparison game or the "I am all alone" pitfall keep you from sharing the perspective that someone needs to hear. Your story is your story for a reason, and impact is at your fingertips. Of all people, you are the most worthy to share your story.

Today, I encourage you to put down this book and sit in silence for just a couple minutes. There is a section in the Victorious Workbook that is designed for you to write down your story in whatever way you desire. Feel free to grab your own notepad if you would prefer that instead. In the workbook, however, there are prompts to help you recall things you would like to share with others.

Looking back at other exercises in your workbook, recall the battle cry you stated and what you have overcome. Next, start thinking about the lessons you have learned or areas you have grown as you have lived with a chronic illness. What would you tell your younger self as encouragement or something you wish you knew then? As those lessons come to memory, jot down some of your memories of diagnoses, surgeries, doctors' visits, etc.

These are some of the base prompts to get you started as you formulate your story with pen and paper. Isn't it so freeing to recall some of those things and think through the intricacies of your story? I know writing this book was both nostalgic and healing for me as I processed the events I had already gone through with my CHD. There were definite times during my writing I had to pause for a moment because of the memories and emotions it brought up, but I am so grateful for that journey. It has made me love myself and my story ten times more.

I know that as you share your story, you will be even more in awe of the things you have overcome. A healthy admiration, you could call it. And rightly so! It's your victory story!

*Chapter 16*

———ᘉᗷᘉᗷᗢᘉᗷᗢᘉᗷ———

# WELCOME TO YOUR VICTORY STORY

C an I just say how proud I am of you and how grateful I am that you have chosen my book to invest your time in? Not only am I so excited to hear how you share your story, but I fully know how capable and worthy you are to inspire others with your incredible victory story. It is by no means an easy journey when you have a chronic illness, but when you continue to live life each day with a victory mindset, you are living as your full and truest self. A self that doesn't view their chronic illness or themselves as a limit, label, or burden but rather an opportunity for relationship and impact.

My senior year of high school, I took a personal finance course, which to this day is my favorite class I have ever taken. It's where I discovered my love for finance and business and truly my love for learning. I ate up that class and admired my teacher, Mr. Peterson, greatly for the way he fueled this interest of mine. At the end of the year, I received an award for that class, and when Mr. Peterson called me up to receive the award, he said some words I have never forgotten: "Victoria, I know that whatever you choose to do in life, you will be successful." That admonition has stuck with me since that award ceremony through the challenging times of navigating college, career paths, and owning a business today. Sometimes it takes one little sentence like that to stick with you for the rest of your life. So I want to give you the same admonition as well. Because I know that whatever you do, you are resilient, my friend, and you will be successful wherever life takes you because of it!

I thank you again for letting me be a part of your chronic illness story. It is such a privilege that I hold to be able to share my story with you, and I hope that it has left you feeling heard and inspired. If you know of other women in your friend circles or in your family that are affected by a chronic illness, I would love for you to share this book with them. If you are wanting to be a part of a larger community of other women living and thriving with a chronic illness, you can go to my website at www.torijoygeiger.com/victorious and join the TJG Victory Tribe Facebook Group. This closed Facebook Group is a chance for us women to lift each other up and offer encouragement and community to fellow sisters on similar paths. What better way to share our stories than together, right? I'd love to see you there, victory friend!

# Final Thoughts

From the time I was born to the present, I have had so many tremendous experiences. I have had to overcome a lot of difficulties and roadblocks, but I have not had to do it alone. God has been there every step of the way. I have learned a lot about my faith through all these experiences. A mentor of mine emailed me an article the other day that said, "Faith is taking God at His Word."[15] For me, that is the best way to describe my faith. Many use the verse Hebrews 11:1 to describe faith: "Now faith is confidence in what we hope for and assurance about what we do not see."[16] That is an excellent way to portray it too, but when I think about defining faith as taking God at His Word, it reminds me that no matter how I feel about a circumstance or what the circumstance is about, God's

---

[15]  Adrian Rogers, "Faith…taking God at His Word," Love Worth Finding Ministries, October 25, 2017, https://www. lwf.org/daily-devotions/faith-taking-god-at-his-word.

[16]  *Bible Hub*, *Bible Hub*, 2004, https://biblehub.com/niv/hebrews/11.htm.

promises remain. His Word found in Scripture stays true. His love and grace stay true. When your whole world seems to be caving in or when your identity is shaken, you can find stability in God's Word that forever remains.

Looking back, there are all these tiny intricacies in my story. If I had done something slightly different in life, my life would not be the same.

He brought my name to life as I grew up. It has a deeper meaning because of my story. When the doctors warned my parents about the problems I could have mentally or the physical problems that could occur, He designed me to be the unique athlete I am today to show them His power. When my mother's OBGYN advised her to "do something about her pregnancy," suggesting abortion, God revealed the meaning and purpose in one of the smallest forms of life.

Because of His grace, I have learned to live victoriously through His love. Despite my anger or misunderstanding of His work in my life, He has always remained. The incident my freshman year of high school was no accident. He was adding to my story of victory.

I am so blessed that I had the opportunity to play volleyball in college, but if I had not transferred to George Fox, I would have never ran track and won an NCAA Northwest Conference championship with an amazing track team, or won an individual women's high jump title. If I had never done track at Fox, I would not have met the man of my dreams, my husband Devin. My relationship with my brother, Grant, may have not grown to be as strong as it is today. Through my opportunities at Fox, I developed my passion even more for business, and especially for the field of accounting and finance, and had the amazing privileges of starting companies at such a young age. That's why God's in charge.

I hope that you see in all those examples that God's fingerprints were all over the decisions and routes in my life. Those are just a few examples, and I can definitely admit that amidst the storms and the difficult decision of transferring colleges, I did not see the silver lining or how God would still transform areas of my life. The encouraging thing is, He is not done with me or my story yet either! I am so overwhelmed with joy when I think about that!

I am not claiming to have life figured out. Not even close. But I can honestly say that choosing to live victoriously through Christ, my Lord and Savior, has been the best decision of my life, one that surpasses any championship.

If after reading this book, you have seen the love and power of Jesus Christ, but you have not personally committed your life to a relationship with Him, I invite you to read the prayer below, and ask Jesus into your heart today. You will not regret it.

And lastly, remember that through Christ you will *always* be victorious!

Blessings,
Tori Joy Geiger

*Prayer*

Dear God,

You have given my life a story.

You created me, and you love me.

You loved me so much, you sent your son to die on the cross for my salvation.

Today, I accept you into my heart.

I want a personal relationship with you, and from this day forward, I want you to be a part of my story.

# Bibliography

Alano, Lindsay, and Tamika Decatur. Fear-A Driving Force. Other. *Navigating The True North*, September 24, 2019. https://podcasts.apple.com/pl/podcast/navigating-the-true-north/id1469489916.

*Bible Hub*, 2004. https://biblehub.com/niv/galatians/3.htm.

*Bible Hub*, 2004. https://biblehub.com/niv/hebrews/11.htm.

*Bible Hub*, 2004. https://biblehub.com/niv/james/1.htm.

*Bible Hub*, 2004. https://biblehub.com/niv/proverbs/31.htm.

*Bible Hub*, 2004. https://biblehub.com/niv/psalms/23.htm.

*Bible Hub*, 2004. https://biblehub.com/niv/psalms/46.htm.

Buffini, Brian. Overcoming Adversity – an Interview with Dick Hoyt #274. Other. *The Brian Buffini Show*, April 20, 2021. https://www.thebrianbuffinishow.com/overcoming-adversity-an-interview-with-dick-hoyt-274/.

Clear, James. *Atomic Habits: An Easy & Proven Way to Build Good Habits & Break Bad Ones*. New York City, NY: Avery Publishing Group, 2018.

Duckworth, Angela. *Grit: The Power of Passion and Perseverance*. New York City, NY: Scribner, 2018.

ELROD, HAL. *MIRACLE Equation: The Two Decisions That Move Your Biggest Goals from Possible, TO Probable, to... Inevitable*. S.l.: JOHN MURRAY LEARNING, 2020.

March of Dimes. "Congenital Heart Defects and Critical Chds." March of Dimes, June 2019. https://www.marchofdimes.org/complications/congenital-heart-defects.aspx#:~:text=Nearly%201%20in%20100%20babies,or%20can%20be%20treated%20easily.

McNamara, Sean, Sean McNamara, David Zelon, Douglas Schwartz, Douglas Schwartz, Dutch Hofstetter, David Brookwell, Deborah Schwartz, and Michael Berk. *Soul Surfer*. DVD. United States: TriStar Pictures, 2011.

Rogers, Adrian. "Faith...taking God at His Word." Love Worth Finding Ministries, October 25, 2017. https://www. lwf.org/daily-devotions/faith-taking-god-at-his-word.

*Where the Red Fern Grows*. VHS. United States: Crown International Pictures, 1974.

# Acknowledgements

**B**ehind every victory story is an incredible support system, and I cannot express how much gratitude is in my heart toward my amazing friends, family, teammates, and mentors through the years. As I end this book, I have to write a few words of thanks to those who have truly impacted my life. I could spend a majority of this book just thanking everyone involved.

Mom and Dad, you instilled in me a confidence and bravery to embrace every moment in life, whether joyful or trying. To you, I will always be beyond grateful.

Grant, my amazing brother, thank you for always being my biggest role model and fan throughout the years. You have been my day-one best friend.

Devin, my wonderful husband, you never cease to inspire me and keep a smile on my face. Thank you for always supporting my dreams, challenging me to be the best I can be, and loving me through all my crazy ideas!

Thank you to everyone who has been with me from the beginning of my story. Your prayers, encouragement, and support will never be forgotten. I love you all!

# NOW IT'S YOUR TURN
**Want to get your story PUBLISHED?**

Self-Publishing School helped me, and now
I want them to help you with this FREE
resource to begin outlining your book**!**

Even if you're busy, bad at writing, or don't
know where to start, you CAN write a
bestseller and build your best life.

With tools and experience across a variety of niches
and professions, Self-Publishing School is the <u>only</u>
resource you need to take your book to the finish line!

## DON'T WAIT

Say "YES" to telling your story!

https://self-publishingschool.com/friend/

Follow the steps on the page to get a FREE resource
to get started on your book and unlock a discount
to get started with Self-Publishing School.

# About the Author

Tori Geiger is from the wine country area of Newberg, Oregon, and lives there with her husband, Devin, and adorable goldendoodle, Teddy. She is a passionate entrepreneur and has owned multiple businesses serving a variety of needs from the time she graduated college in 2019.

Tori is a congenital heart defect survivor and has undergone multiple open-heart surgeries and procedures throughout her life. Growing up, she was an avid athlete, participating in volleyball, basketball, and track in high school. She went on to play volleyball at Corban University and later join the track team at George Fox University as a high jumper.

With a heart for others affected by chronic illnesses such as CHD, Tori started a lifestyle blog where she shares lifestyle and chronic illness tips. Part of her mission is to have a "heart that beats for others," and to help others achieve the same. Tori does this through her 50/50 CHD Promise; 50% of her blogging commissions are donated to CHD organizations.

When Tori is not blogging or running her businesses, she loves traveling, cooking with her hubby, running, and paddleboarding. *From Vulnerable to Victorious* is Tori's first book.

# Can You Help?

**Thank you for reading my book!**

I really appreciate all of your feedback, and
I love hearing what you have to say.

I need your input to make the next version
of this book and my future books better.

Please leave me an honest review on Amazon
letting me know what you thought of the book.

Thanks so much!

Tori Joy Geiger

Made in the USA
Monee, IL
12 October 2021